HE.CE.2004
SW

THE TROUBLED MIND OF
NORTHERN IRELAND

THE TROUBLED MIND
OF
NORTHERN IRELAND

An Analysis of the Emotional Effects
of the Troubles

Raman Kapur
Jim Campbell

KARNAC

LONDON   NEW YORK

First published in 2004 by
H. Karnac (Books) Ltd.
6 Pembroke Buildings, London NW10 6RE

British Library Cataloguing in Publication Data

A C.I.P. for this book is available from the British Library

ISBN 1 85575 993 4

Edited, designed and produced by The Studio Publishing Services Ltd, Exeter EX4 8JN

Printed in Great Britain

10 9 8 7 6 5 4 3 2 1

www.karnacbooks.com

CONTENTS

FOREWORD

Killing human beings is an unpleasant affair. What is of concern in the world today is how the human mind can be persuaded that taking another life is a good idea. In this book, Kapur and Campbell apply a particular model of psychology, Kleinian psychoanalysis, to illustrate how the sane and civilized part of all of our human minds can be hijacked to be part of the most ghastly of deeds. The central message of the book is the humanization rather than the demonization of human relationships. The authors urge us to think about the human cost of inflicting destruction on other people; from words to the deadly act of taking someone's life. They emphasize that we all have a part to play, no matter how high in the pecking order we may be.

If leaders in society think about how their words could be used to justify hate, they could lessen the possibility of those lower in the pecking order embarking on verbal and physical acts of destruction. Kapur and Campbell emphasize the importance of people power; taking responsibility for the way we relate in everyday life to create a culture of humanity rather than insanity. Insanity, for them, is treating people as less than human beings, as statistics that are reported in the news and then forgotten the very next day.

Statistics are human beings, irrespective of colour and position; they are mothers, fathers, husbands, and wives to other human beings. Importantly, tthe authors emphasize the difference between bad guilt and good guilt. Good guilt is when you realize you have done bad things to others and there is a genuine wish to repair and develop the important capacity for concern.

Kapur and Campbell have written this book for the professional, the politician, and ordinary people in the street. In drawing on their personal experiences in Northern Ireland they give us a model for understanding human destruction that can be universally applied. Maybe in our troubled world of today we can apply these experiences from Northern Ireland to make our world a safer and happier place to live.

Archbishop Tutu
June 2004

Raman Kapur is Director of the mental health charity, THRESHOLD, and a consultant clinical psychologist and psychoanalytic psycho-therapist. He has published clinical and research papers in the field of individual and group psychotherapy and has a particular interest in bringing psychoanalytic ideas into the public domain to understand everyday life, particularly terrorism and trauma. He is a broadcaster for local radio in Northern Ireland and also holds an honorary senior lectureship with Queens University Belfast.

Jim Campbell is a senior lecturer in the School of Social Work, Queens University Belfast, having previously worked as a mental health social worker in Northern Ireland. He has recently published in the field of mental health law, mental health social work, and the impact of the Northern Irish conflict upon practice, and is interested in exploring ways in which analytical perspectives can be used to understand the "Troubles".

INTRODUCTION

"The first evil choice or act is linked to the second; and each one to
the one that follows, both by the tendency of our evil nature and by
the power of habit, which holds us by destiny"
    Goldberg (1996) *Speaking with the Devil. A Dialogue with Evil*
    (Viking, New York, p. 209)

Viktor Frankl, an eminent psychotherapist, described his experiences in a concentration camp in terms of the "abnormal becoming
normal", an inevitable result of being exposed to destructive, violent processes. A concern for "the other" becomes replaced with
hostility and a lack of compassion for our fellow human beings.
There are many examples of such catastrophic events in the history
of the world, and we continue to witness the consequences of systems of social, political, and economic oppression, in the last few
years in places like Bosnia, Rwanda, and currently in the Middle
East.

And so to Northern Ireland. In our recent "Troubles" (a local
term that somehow understates the violence), over 1.5 million
human beings have been exposed to death and destructiveness
for a sustained period of over thirty years. When you do bad things

to people bad things happen. Humanity becomes replaced with barbarism. Life becomes cheap. As in other places around the world, people are dehumanized, often simply represented in statistics, and quickly forgotten about as we try to move on and make sense of the world in which we live.

So how can we increase our understanding of these processes and discuss the conditions under which people may be more able to relate to each other in humane rather than destructive ways? This book is a modest attempt to answer some of these complex questions, using perspectives that we hope are novel and that can add to the existing body of literature on the Troubles to date. Of course, the way we build up our views on the world is contingent upon many factors, not least the way we have grown up, witnessed, and processed events that surround us in our everyday lives. Both authors have sought to understand how and why the abnormality and violence of many aspects of life in Northern Ireland have become normal, but from different personal and professional standpoints.

Raman Kapur grew up in a semi-rural part of Northern Ireland as a member of a small ethnic community. He left Northern Ireland to study and practise clinical psychology in Blackburn and London and was particularly influenced by Kleinian psychoanalysis, an approach that sought to unravel the habitual nature of day-to-day hostile human relationships. On his return to Northern Ireland some years later, it became apparent to him that such an approach may be useful in explaining the way in which human relations have unfolded during the Troubles.

The second author, Jim Campbell, grew up in Belfast and has lived with the Troubles for most of his life. As a social worker and a social work educator, he is interested not just in the social and political dimensions of the conflict, but in the way in which wider social structures impact on the individual, whether they are clients or professionals. The work of Klein and object relations theorists provides a refreshing alternative, or addition, to existing ideas about the Troubles in Northern Ireland.

To date there have been some attempts to use the work of Klein and post-Kleinians in explaining relationships between wider social structures and the psychology of human destructiveness, but very little has been said about how such psychoanalyical approaches can be used in the context of Northern Ireland. To the authors, this conundrum seemed difficult to understand; psychoanalysis, one assumes, should be good at revealing the primitive depths of the human mind that generate such destructive emotions. Thus, the idea of the book was born. We wish the book to be viewed and used in a number of ways. Some aspects introduce the reader to some of the basic tenets of object relations theory, its origins and application in therapeutic milieu, as well as the manner in which it has been extended to allow for the analysis of broader social processes. Because the text is centrally concerned with the Northern Ireland conflict, details of history, society, and politics in this troubled and troublesome region are provided. Perhaps most importantly, we wanted to write about these issues in a way that is readable to as broad a community as possible. So, although we refer to "academic" literature, we also pay attention to popular sources as a way of explaining our ideas and their applicability.

The manner in which the book is constructed follows these aspirations. The first chapter outlines the political background to the Troubles, describing the structure of a society and the national and international factors that have led to manifestations of violence and hate.

Chapter Two describes the framework for Kleinian psychoanalysis, which provides an understanding of how human destructiveness can be fixed in the "paranoid–schizoid" position. Also described are the processes required to move to a more healthy "depressive position", an unfortunate title that, in essence, represents the capacity for concern for another human being.

Chapter Three applies these concepts to the troubled society of Northern Ireland, and highlights how day-to-day societal human relations are infected by destructive processes. In this and subsequent chapters the first author (RK) particularly draws on his own experiences to understand specific states of mind.

Chapter Four uses quotations from the writings of "terrorists" about their life of hate to describe the effect of the Troubles on individuals, while Chapter Five takes an overview of group processes in a troubled society, drawing on the work of Wilfred Bion.

Chapter Six focuses on the effects of the Troubles on the state of mind of professionals working with those affected by trauma. This is of particular interest to both authors, who work in the field of mental health and social care.

Finally, Chapter Seven brings these themes together and points to psychological and emotional pre-conditions of any peace process to move from a troubled mind to a mind at peace with itself. Political processes are ineffective without a parallel process that addresses the fixed and chronic states of mind that maintain people relating to each other in a destructive and evil way.

CHAPTER ONE

Politics, violence, and the management of conflict in Northern Ireland

I t does not seem possible to understand fully the emotional and psychological well-being of the people who live in Northern Ireland without first considering the nature of the state and society that have often been described as the most violent in western Europe. Since the advent of the most recent "Troubles" in 1969, over 3,600 people have died, and tens of thousands have suffered physical, psychological, and emotional injury as a result of inter-communal, paramilitary, and state violence. If these figures were to be extrapolated for the population of Britain, then close to 150,000 people would have died and millions would have been traumatized. It is important to recognize, however, the nature of the "ebb and flow" of the conflict; in the early to mid 1970s no-warning bomb explosions and sectarian murders were commonplace. During this period around half of all deaths occurred. Since then, deaths caused by the Troubles have gradually declined, with the notable exceptions of years in which violence erupted because of the shifting political processes or events created by protagonists to the conflict (Fay *et al.*, 1999).

Of course, the Troubles are not a new phenomenon in this part of the world. Many people of a certain age in Northern Ireland have been told stories by their parents or grandparents about the awful events of an early period of Troubles in the 1920s, when hundreds of people, the majority of them Catholic, were murdered around the time of the partition of Ireland. Even before this important political watershed, the history of Ireland was often characterized by violence and oppression, particularly following the period of colonialization described in the literature as the Plantation (Bardon, 2001). The subsequent 400 years, which led to the partition of Ireland, can be interpreted in various ways, but usually in terms of struggles over religious and national identities or socio-economic positions (McGarry & O'Leary, 1996).

It was The Government of Ireland Act, 1920 that partitioned Ireland and left the north eastern six counties a contested geopolitical space that is the backdrop to the modern Troubles in Northern Ireland. Since 1921 many Catholics, who constituted a large minority (one third) of the population of Northern Ireland, perceived themselves as nationalists who had been "trapped" and became increasingly fearful that their political aspirations to be part of the new Republic of Ireland in the southern twenty-six counties were not going to be fully recognized. On the other hand, most Protestants (around one million) saw the union with the United Kingdom as a guarantee of their civil and political rights, and felt threatened by what appeared to be an alien and hostile culture in the south. Simplistic notions of national identity, religious affiliation, and ethnic difference cannot, however, fully explain the history of the political conflict in Northern Ireland. There have been various moments in this history when nationality and sectarian head-counting have not been the organizing principles around which politics revolve. For example, the motivation of class interests can partly explain the revolt of the United Irishmen in 1798, the Poor Law Relief riots in Belfast in 1933, and the rise of the Northern Ireland Labour Party in the 1960s.

It has been argued that the extensive use of ethnopolitical analyses in the study of the Northern Irish conflict has often overshadowed the value of class as a critical concept in understanding the Troubles (Coulter, 1999). The nature of the capitalist formation in the north of Ireland created the conditions for sectarian conflict and exploitation of working-class communities. Inequalities of class remain marked and visible in contemporary society. When we examine the statistics of death and injury caused by the Troubles, working-class areas have suffered disproportionately (Fay *et al.*, 1999) and the region has been classified as one of high social and economic need under the European Union Anti-Poverty Programme. Yet many middle-class people experience a high standard of living because of, or despite, the conflict. The establishment of the non-sectarian Alliance Party in the early 1970s, followed by the politicization of paramilitary groupings in the 1980s and 1990s, and added to by new parties such as the Women's Coalition, suggests greater diversity at political and civic levels and a new, allbeit limited, willingness to challenge the causes of such inequalities. It is also important not to discount the role of social movements, however much they are marginalized, in influencing politics and society in Northern Ireland. The unfortunate conclusion that can be drawn from these figures is that voices seeking to challenge the dominant ideologies, whether they are Republican and Nationalist or Loyalist and Unionist, tend to struggle to be heard.

In addition to these internal processes there are, of course, many external factors that have influenced the course of the Troubles. For example, Republican groups have been particularly dependent on funding from a range of interested parties in the United States of America, and a pattern of strong cultural links continues to exist between Northern Ireland and North America for both communities. Paramilitary links have been formed between Republicans and Libya, Palestine, and the Basque region of Spain, while Loyalists have bonds with South Africa and Israel. The entrance of the United Kingdom and the Republic of Ireland into the European Union has also led to many political, social, and economic projects designed to solve aspects of the conflict. It should be also be recognized that these two key nation states themselves have helped, but sometimes hindered, opportunities for conflict resolution in Northern Ireland (Gaffikin & Morrissey, 1990; Whyte, 1991).

These many, complex factors help to explain the inherent instability of the state in Northern Ireland and the failure of attempts to resolve the conflict that has scarred this society. The politics of the first fifty years were marked by tension between the injustices, real and perceived, which many Nationalists felt, and the hopes and fears of a largely Protestant, Unionist majority that possessed almost total control of political and adminstrative powers of state.

Disregard by Westminster of the internal affairs of Northern Ireland since its inception in 1921 allowed a politics typified by different forms of discrimination, particularly sectarianism (McVeigh, 1997). Even since the central government in Westminster took full responsibility for the administration of Northern Ireland in 1972, a debate has ensued about whether discrimination has been alleviated. For example, existing fair employment legislation has done little in changing the disadvantaged position of Catholics in the labour market. Explanations involving both indirect and direct discrimination have been used to explain why Catholics are more than twice as likely as Protestants to be unemployed (McGarry & O'Leary, 1996; Teague, 1993). At the same time it is important to avoid simplistic judgements about such inequalities. There is evidence to suggest that many Protestant communities have lived through and suffered from the sort of abject poverty Catholics experienced during this period.

These complex social and political relationships help to explain why Northern Ireland is often viewed as a "place apart" within the United Kingdom. Although constitutionally part of the UK, since its inception in 1921 the region has continually experienced long periods of social and political unrest. Attempts by the central state to establish a sense of "normal" social and political life in the last seventy-five years have largely failed because the core concepts of nationhood and citizenship have been contested both within and outside Northern Ireland, and because of mismanagement and neglect by Westminster. Arguably the most corrosive manifestation of this crisis of state has been problematic nature of law security and policing.

The economic and social manifestations of a troubled society

Despite its relatively prosperous history and location in relation to the rest of the island, the decline of traditional industry, punctuated by the two world wars, left Northern Ireland's economy weak for most of the twentieth century (Borooah, 1993). This enduring history of economic decline and social exclusion is reflected in the health, social, and educational policies. After the second world war the Unionist administration decided to follow some of the policies outlined by the Beveridge Plan in Britain. There were political reasons for this choice, in particular the opportunity to use social policy to reinforce a common notion of Britishness as well as enhancing the sense of difference and advantage in comparison with the rudimentary system of welfare regime which existed in the south of the island. Apart from these ideological motives there seems little doubt that economic necessity implied necessary changes to social policy. Since its inception, Northern Ireland has always been dependent on subventions from the Westminster government in order to deliver upon a wide range of spending commitments in social security, health and education, agriculture, industry, and security. The precariousness of the declining Northern Irish economy only served to reinforce this perception of dependency.

The political economy of Northern Ireland, since 1921, has been characterized by high levels of unemployment, poverty, and a range of unmet social and health needs. Although the economy has grown noticeably during the last decade, rates of long-term unemployment, dependence on benefits, and food and heating costs remain high by UK standards, while income from paid employment remains relatively low (Northern Ireland Abstract of Statistics (NIAS), 2003, p. 122). When these figures are disaggregated we find that men are more likely to be unemployed than women and Catholics more likely to be unemployed than Protestants. People living "west of the Bann" (mostly Catholics) are more likely to be socially excluded from employment and to suffer from poor housing. The demographic structure of Northern Ireland may also affect the quality of life. There are now nearly 1.7 million people in a region which has a higher birth rate and thus higher rate of natural increase than the UK average, although it has been estimated that there will be some convergence with the UK average as the century moves on. The apparent stability of family life in Northern Ireland is often commented upon by policy makers. Even though births outside marriage continue to rise, they are still less than the UK average and divorce rates are low. However, there are higher rates of lone parenthood and numbers of young in Northern Ireland.

The traditionally high rates of migration out of Northern Ireland may explain why the society remains static and inward-looking, and a number of factors might have accounted for this—poor employment prospects, political conflict, and a shortage of places for students in higher education. However, recent political developments and an expanding economy might explain a trend towards inward migration (NIAS, 2003, p. 15). It is noticeable that these changes have increased the awareness and visibility of ethnic minority groups. In the past it was often mistakenly assumed by policy makers and the wider public that issues of racism (in contrast to the conflicts over religious and national affiliation) did not exist in what was apparently a homogenous society. We now realize that a substantial traditional ethnic minority in the form of the travelling community has always lived in this part of the world, and been discriminated against over the centuries. In addition, the numbers of "new" ethnic minority communities living in Northern Ireland have grown significantly in recent years. It is some indication of the "colour-blindness" of Northern Irish society that it has taken so long for race relations legislation to be introduced (Hainsworth, 1998).

Perhaps unsurprisingly, given the contested nature of life and citizenship in Northern Ireland, housing has been a contentious issue; public housing has in the past involved maladministration and is a central factor in ongoing intercommunal strife. Housing policy has been subject to much debate in Northern Ireland, both before and during the present "Troubles". It has been argued that the issue of public housing allocation and the associated gerrymandering of votes in elections for local government was the most important factor in the creation of the civil rights movement of the late 1960s, which led eventually to the creation of the Northern Ireland Housing Executive (NIHE) (Gaffikin & Morrissey, 1990). This body was designed to take power away from discredited local politicians and place it in the hands of "neutral" professional bureaucrats. The result has been that the NIHE has had responsibility for many aspects of public and private housing in Northern Ireland during a period of intense civil and political conflict. In the late 1960s the biggest movement of population in Europe since the war took place in the streets of Belfast and other parts of Northern Ireland; these events took place in the midst of sectarian conflict and intimidation. Since then, many areas of housing in Northern Ireland are marked by sectarian, geopolitical boundaries, which makes the NIHE's task of using objective criteria in the allocation

of housing on grounds of priority a difficult one. It has been estimated that over 70% of public housing is segregated (Heenan &
Lloyd, 2002) and even in relatively well-off surburban areas, mixing
can be problematic. Such divisions are reinforced by boundary
markers, explicitly presented or more subtly understated. The
urban landscape of Belfast, for example, is characterized by a patch-
work of village-like communities with discrete living areas for
Catholics and Protestants. In many working-class communities the
flying of national or paramilitary flags and the painting of kerbs
and wall murals denote ownership of territory, symbols of identity,
and a brooding menace to the "other". A critical understanding of
the concept of sectarianism can help help to explain such behaviour
and practices. Sectarianism pervades all aspects of life in Northern
Ireland, at personal, familial, and societal levels. Death and the fear
of death and injury, taken together with the social cleavages created
by the Troubles, have inevitably affected communities in Northern
Ireland. A major difficulty in trying to deal with the fear associated
with sectarianism is the subtle mechanisms that serve to perpetuate
oppression. These include the identification of social markers that
help to make distinctions about "the other"—the family names, the
use of language, the schools attended, the areas lived in. These
social markers help to reinforce stereotypical ideas about Protestant
and Catholic (Brewer, 1991).

There are, however, also positive attributes to the way in which
such communities have preserved and developed political and
cultural identity in the midst of crisis. The changing content and style
of some murals may reflect changing views on politics and history,
sometimes revising folk interpretations of the past and responding
to the challenges of the present and future (Coulter, 1999; Rolston &
Miller, 1996).

As with housing, the educational system both reflects and reinforces sectarian divisions in Northern Ireland. Over 90% of children
are educated in predominantly Catholic or Protestant schools,
although there is a small but growing integrated sector. As in other
areas of social and economic life, the origins of these divisions are
centuries old, but reinforced by the establishment of the devolved
administration in 1921. Both academic and sporting curriculae have
developed to mirror the needs of parallel academic systems, so it is
hardly surprising to find that teachers are trained in separate

colleges, and that, with the exception of soccer, other main sports reflect sectarian divisions. Thus gaelic sports are played mostly by Catholics and rugby, field hockey. and cricket by Protestants (Sugden & Bairner, 1993). Yet within the system of education other social cleavages exist, sometimes hidden and unspoken. Both Catholic and Protestant sectors are characterized by divisions of class and status, largely encouraged by the continuance of academic selection at the age of eleven and a robust and assertive grammar school lobby. This situation has continued in Northern Ireland, despite the fact that elsewhere in the UK comprehensive approaches were introduced in the 1970s (Gallagher & Smith, 2000). Although a great deal is often made about the positive outcomes of the grammar school system, particularly in terms of academic achievement, there is evidence to suggest that, overall, the system is failing many children and families. For example, "A" level and university qualifications remain in and around the UK average while the number of school leavers with no qualifications is exceptionally high (Department for Employment and Learning (DEL), 2003).

A similar picture of inequality emerges when factors of health and health care are considered. There are established correlations between mortality rates and class. In terms of UK averages, Northern Ireland has very high rates of death by heart disease and high rates of some forms of cancer, road traffic deaths, and tranquillizer prescriptions.

Such factors partly explain why spending per capita on health care in Northern Ireland is well above the UK average. The contextual background of the political conflict has served to intensify the interplay between these factors, which have given rise to high levels of both social and economic deprivation; in addition the deregulation of the labour market in Northern Ireland has led to more part-time work and a loss of entitlement to employment protection. Until relatively recently, Northern Ireland has been one of the poorest regions in the UK, a situation that has been partially offset by high levels of public expenditure. There is higher per capita public expenditure in Northern Ireland than in Scotland, England, and Wales. Gaffikin and Morrissey (1990) have argued that a combination of factors—particularly the need to manage political and social conflict—led to relatively high levels of public expenditure during the

"Thatcher years" at a time when financial retrenchment was occurring elsewhere in the UK. Interestingly, this has led to some convergence between Northern Ireland and other poorer regions in the
UK. On the other hand, it can be argued that very high levels of
social and health need, and a massive security budget, explain this
"dependence" on funds from central government.

When Direct Rule was imposed in 1972, the state engaged in a
strategy designed to deliver health and social care in a way it hoped
would avoid discrimination and contribute, at least partly, to the
resolution of social conflict in Northern Ireland. Although there
have been some successful aspects to what has become known as
the "integrated service", often much admired by professionals in the
rest of the UK for its potential for harmonious multi-disciplinary
working, there is also room for criticism. The attempt to technocra-
tize the welfare state has allowed professionals to practise in ways
that are often detached from the communities they seek to serve,
often failing to acknowledge, let alone challenge, sectarianism and
its causes. This is an issue we will return to in Chapter Six.

Politics, society and psychology

So far we have highlighted a number of political, social, and
economic factors that affect the lives of citizens and may help us to
understand how and why the Troubles have persisted. Alongside
this body of literature there exists a growing range of approaches
that seek to deal with the relationship between social and political
events and their impact upon individual and group psyches. For
example, some psychiatrists have sought to establish a relationship
between political violence and mental ill-health. Thus Lyons (1974)
found an unexpected absence of morbid symptomatology following violent incidents. More recent studies (Loughry et al., 1988),
using the post-traumatic stress disorder classification, suggest
the existence of real, although sometimes hidden, psychological
sequalae in the case of patients who experience violence at first
hand. Moving outside the psychiatrist's consulting room, social
psychologists have sought to explore the impact of the Troubles
on the wider population, through community-based studies (Cairns
& Wilson, 1989), or in terms of the behaviour and attitudes of

competing groups and identities (Heskin, 1980). There is much current interest in exploring the impact of violence on various aspects of individual and social life, particularly at this moment when opportunities for conflict resolution seem possible.

Hargie and Dickson (2003), for example, present an overview of the central themes of research into the Troubles over the last thirty-five years. In reviewing the contributions of several researchers in their reference texts, they point to several themes of research so far. First, in highlighting research by the political researchers Darby and McGinty (2003), they point to the universality of such conflicts, whether they are in Northern Ireland, South Africa, the Middle East, or elsewhere. There is a need, they argue, for the diffusion of triumphalism with symbolism and the importance of clear political changes that affect the structure of society. One of the impediments to peace is a socialization process that establishes and reinforces destructive thoughts and behaviour throughout the life cycle. They cite Connolly and Healy (2003) in this respect:

> Connolly and Healy provide an illuminating insight into what is happening in the minds of children at various stages of development. Their findings confirm the fears that sectarian attitudes are taken in by children almost with mothers milk. At the age of three to four years, they had already begun to identify with their "own" signs and symbols (flags, soccer jerseys etc) and were able to identify the other side's symbols and rate these negatively. . . . By the age of seven to eight years, Connolly and Healy show how these attitudes had begun to solidify. At this age children spend much of their time outside the home playing with in-group friends, and the "them and us" socialisation process is reinforced by the peer group. [Hargie & Dickson, 2003, p. 293]

A proposed solution to this process of prejudice creation is suggested by Morrow et al. (2003). They point to societal responsibility, which focuses on the responsibility of everyone, not only those involved in sectarian conflict, to be aware of their own prejudices and stereotypes. Any proposed community relations programmes need to be well thought out and embedded in the real-life experience of groups and communities.

Next, Hargie and Dickson (2003) point to the role of symbols and emblems in perpetuating conflict. In referring to the work of

Darby and McGinty (2003), they highlight the role of symbols as the collective focus of bonds and a shared group identity that also have a territorial quality. However, while providing this group security they provoke hostility from other groups, which can reinforce archaic and hostile ways of resolving conflict. In suggesting solutions to this polarization of symbolization they refer to the suggestion of Morrow *et al.* (2003) that diversity should be embraced, allowing room for everyone to express their own particular identity through symbols and thus trying to minimize the conflict this may create through a deeper acceptance of other traditions. While this is a laudable model of potentially developing a truly pluralistic society, both Morrow and Hargie and Dickson identify the "seismic shifts" that have to take place for these changes to occur.

In their next theme, the authors attempt to draw on the lessons from the interface. In focusing on North Belfast, Murtagh (2003) and Jarman (2003) point to this area of Northern Ireland as being at the very epicentre of the Troubles, accounting for most deaths in the province. The extract below highlights an important characteristic of this particular "patch" of Northern Ireland.

> The communities have become increasingly segregated, with the younger generation being more sectarian in their views than their parents. One reason for this is that many of them have never interacted with the out-group, whereas their parents and grandparents have had at least some experience of the "other side", which serves to moderate their beliefs. [Hargie & Dickson, 2003, pp. 300–3001]

A solution these researchers suggest is to provide a proactive and coordinated approach to minimizing segregation, so giving each side a chance to become less polarized.

Bloomer and Weinreich (2003) underscore the importance of identity formation on influencing attitudes and behaviour. This is a complex problem that does not easily fall into separate categories of Catholic and Protestant groupings. These researchers found further differentiations within their own communities, with Protestants displaying less of a single entity than Catholics. They also found some evidence of middle-class religious groupings distancing themselves from the sectarianism of working-class groups.

Overall, the picture of religious and political identity may be more complex than it appears.

On the issue of leadership, Gormley-Heenan and Robinson (2003) comment on how a peace process was initiated in Northern Ireland when, in substance, most of the political leaders remained the same. They comment on leadership pre-1980 being characterized as under-developed, intimidatory, factional, and demonic. They note changes in how real power became possible through devolution, the influence of external players such as the USA, which encouraged more positive leadership models, and how political leadership became less defined on individuals and more on broader issues. In particular, they note the emergence of smaller political parties such as the Progressive Unionist Party (PUP) and Northern Ireland Women's Coalition (NIWC) as being representative of such change. In essence, their analysis is optimistic, holding out hope for a broader, more pluralistic, approach to leadership in a divided community. Finally, on the issue of sectarianism, Hargie and Dickson (2003) point to comments made by many of their contributors on the rigid and chronic modes of relating characterized by the sectarian nature of Northern Irish society.

We believe that the diversity of theories which are referred to by Hargie and Dickson offer interesting and insightful views on the relationship between the psychology of everyday life and wider social structures. Yet, with few exceptions (Benson, 1992; 1994), psychoanalytic ideas have not been used to understand the relationship between culture, social, and political conflict and the internal world of the psyche. In the analysis that follows, we use object relations theory to explore the nature of social polarization in Northern Ireland and to explain how human relationships are often demonized. At the same time, we wish to discuss how different ways of relating can lead to the humanization of everyday life, an important proposition given the possibilities for change that the current political process is offering.

A framework for understanding troubled relations: the work of Klein and object relations theorists

Introduction

In the previous chapter we described and analysed the complex factors that help to explain the origins and continuance of the present conflict in Northern Ireland. It was acknowledged that a range of theories has been used to understand the violence of the Troubles, but, rather strangely, little has been written (Benson, 1992, 1994) about how psychoanalytical ideas might help us in this area. We believe this to be unusual because there is a long history of the influence of psychoanalytical thought across many fields of human inquiry, including sociology, politics and literature. In this chapter we want to begin to redress this gap, at least partially, by identifying the work of Klein and post-Kleinians as a potential theory base for understanding aspects of the Troubles.

A conceptual framework for understanding human relations

We wake up in the morning and wonder whether we are going to have a good day. Immediately we are thinking about how we relate to ourselves and others. If we have a partner are we opening the day in a good mood? Did we have sex last night? Have we dreamt about things that are on our mind? If we take time to reflect on such events, we begin to appreciate the fundamental importance of human relations to everyday life. One way of conceptualizing at least some aspects of these processes is to appreciate that many such events involve a consideration of how our perception of ourselves and others influences action. For example, the series of activities that encompass every day are often shaped by whether we like or dislike ourselves and others. This very basic division of relationships into good (denoted by constructive, creative actions) and bad (denoted by destructive and deadly actions) is fundamental to a theory of human relationships developed by the psychoanalyst, Melanie Klein (Mitchell, 1986). Figure 1 summarizes a framework and concepts that she developed, which is often referred to as "object relations theory".

Essentially, this model gives us a simple blueprint from which we can begin to think about what we do to ourselves and others. This element of reflection is crucial; too often in life we let relationships pass by at a furious pace and we do not allow ourselves to have moments to sit back and consider these events. If we can learn to think about how and why we harm ourselves and other people, then we can find ways of addressing the anxieties and fears of everyday life. Although there is an understandable belief that psychoanalytical ideas refer essentially to individual thoughts and actions, the work of Klein and others suggest that human judgements are contingent upon a mixture of factors including wider social relationships outside the intra- and inter-psychic world. The following section briefly outlines the historical and theoretical

	SELF	OTHERS
GOOD	KIND	FRIENDSHIP
	BENEVOLENT	
BAD	SELF-HATRED	ENEMIES

Figure 1. Model of human relations.

origins of these concepts and offers an easy-to-use guide as to how they can be applied in everyday relationships.

A history of psychoanalytical ideas

As we know, the origins of psychoanalytical thought lie in the work of Sigmund Freud. Arguably his greatest contribution to our understanding of human behaviour and relations was his suggestion that there existed powerful hidden forces within us that drive us to do things we are not aware of. These unconscious drives are, by definition, very difficult to understand because we are cannot have any awareness of those parts of ourselves about which we have no knowledge. Paradoxically, critics find this the most exasperating aspect of Freud's ideas; it seems speculative and difficult to prove.

The traditional way of uncovering these hidden forces is through personal therapy on the couch. Having identified the possible sources of what makes us anxious about the social world, Freud went on to suggest how the "unconscious could be made conscious". Traditionally, this involves the patient saying the first things that come into his or her mind. The therapist then attempts to understand the meaning of these "free associations" and so the unconscious is explored. Freud's emphasis was very much on understanding the patient in the context of childhood experiences and how these are repeated on to the therapist. This historical reconstruction is seen as critical to this "talking cure" (Greenson, 1967).

It remains debatable as to whether everybody needs, or would benefit from, personal therapy, but we want to suggest here that some of the ideas used in the psychoanalytical tradition may be useful outside the therapist's clinic; it may even be possible to apply some of the theory to yourself, and thus become more aware of yourself and others. In reflecting on your emotional life you may be able to prevent yourself getting into negative relations with yourself and others.

It is at this point that we wish to discuss, in some detail, the work of Melanie Klein, a psychoanalyst who worked before and after the Second World War (1920–1975). From her own personal analysis and her work with children, she changed the focus of analysis from the earlier Freudian attention to past history to the here and now relationship between the therapist and the patient (Bahia, 1981). For Klein the essence of the talking cure is in the quality of human relations between the patient and others, not in the childhood reconstruction of how the person came to be the way he or she is. This fundamental revolution in psychoanalytic theory is called "object relations theory", where object stands for "human". One can trace the tradition of object relations theory from her original work (Klein, 1921, 1926, 1927, 1928, 1932, 1935, 1940–1946) through the publications by Bion (1957, 1958, 1959a,b, 1962), Segal (1973, 1981–1985), Joseph (1980), Spillius (1988a,b) Riesenberg-Malcolm (1999), and Mitrani (2001). Two key concepts remained constant despite the variety of perspectives that have influenced the development of object relations theory. These are described and discussed as follows.

Paranoid–schizoid position

Paula Heimann, a psychoanalyst who followed Klein, wrote:

> Psychopathology of everyday life abounds in examples of paranoid delusions. We are all apt to feel at times, that it always rains when we have planned to spend a day out of doors, that the bus going in the opposite direction to ours always comes first, that some unfortunate experience we have had was directly due to somebody's will or at least to fate. Usually, however, this type of paranoid delusion is easily corrected. On second thoughts we remember many occasions when the weather was kind, when our bus came immediately, or even when we were particularly lucky and we know that our unpleasant experiences are not caused by enemies, personal or impersonal, but result from other factors, including our own errors of judgement and other imperfections. [Heimann, 1955, p. 240]

In this description of how many of us feel when things seem to be going against us, Heimann points to the capacity of most people to find ways of recovering from their pessimism. Difficult moments are usually contained and limited by the arrival of more positive thoughts that prevent a malignant growth into deeper emotional suspicion and mistrust of the world. However, this emotional barrier is not present all of the time and a negative spiralling can take place. In the same text Heimann writes

> Following this line of thought we come to discern a rising scale of severity in delusional attitudes. There is the momentary reaction— "Damn that fool!" Ascending the scale, there is the mood which many persist for some hours "I knew everything would go wrong with me today and it has!" Neither of these leads, as yet, to harmful consequences; both are entirely compatible with sound mental health. Next in severity might be a paranoid state lasting for days or weeks or more. Finally, there is the psychosis in which the person's life is totally determined by his belief in a persecution, the delusion having become permanent, and the focus of a rigid system. [Heimann, 1956, p. 240]

This negative spiralling creates such distrust that the person feels isolated and withdrawn from the world. This distrust becomes the symptom of human destructiveness. Object relations theorists seek to explain this pattern of thought in terms of a model of human development in which early experiences between the mother and the infant are critical. Theoretically, it is proposed that the infant comes into the world with a bundle of life and death instincts. The willingness to live propels the infant to human relatedness, particularly with the mother (but also sometimes with other "good" objects). Psychologists and psychoanalysts have been aware of the importance of this mother–infant bonding for some time. For example, Gooch (1991), in her analysis of how early experiences in the mother–infant couple can affect adult sexuality, writes:

> Harlow's (1961) classic research on rhesus monkeys confirmed the effect of deprivation of a "contact comfort" type of mother love upon adult sexual behaviour. Comparing Harlow's monkeys with his own studies of deprived human infants, Spitz (1962) observed that infants deprived of normal maternal affections showed an absence of genital play and usual autoerotic masturbatory activity— recognised as significant for the development of adult sexuality. Spitz concluded, on the basis of Harlow's and his own findings, that "something" takes place in the normal object relations between mother and infant in both species that implements the libidinal drive in the formal of genital (sexual) behaviour. I am proposing that the "something" which seems to function as a "lock and key" to

the new born infant's future psychosexual maturity is related to the importance of sensual and sexual arousal of both infant and mother in what is called the "original primal scene" in which the infant is an active participant in a mutual overtly erotic relationship with its mother and her breast. [Gooch, 1991, p. 256]

What Gooch and other psychoanalysts have argued is that the intimacy, warmth, and sexuality of the very earliest of human relationships have a profound influence on future social life. This concept of "coupling" then applies to all our relationships with others. Sexual intercourse is a metaphor for human intercourse, with one parallelling the other. It is unlikely that people who lack a fulfilling, satisfying, and mutually dependent sexual relationship will lead fulfilling emotional and personal lives. This notion of coupling analysis is a theoretical proposition that may be criticized for its generalizing nature, but it is one which Kleinians hold dear.

In Freud's ideas, these relationships are expressions of the life instinct, or Eros, but there also exist the more sinister forces of the death instinct (Thanatos) which, in object relations theory, can only be modified by the containing function of the mother. In Kleinian theory the primacy of the mother is particularly recognized as (usually) the first object the infant makes human contact with, but it is sometimes possible that other good objects may fulfil similar functions. At this mother–infant interface the infant is also exposed to external reality. What emerges is a growing realization of a tremendous internal anxiety about the possibility that warmth, love, and feeding may be compromised as the months and years pass. It is at the "synaptic junction" between infant and mother that crucial psychological processes are hypothesized to occur that have a significant impact on our personalities into adult life. Segal (1985) describes this as follows:

When faced with the anxiety produced by the death instinct, the ego deflects it. The deflection of the death instinct, described by Freud, in Melanie Klein's view consists partly of projection, partly of the conversion of the death instinct into aggression . . . the breast, which is felt to contain a great part of the infant's death instinct, is felt to be bad and threatening to the ego, giving rise to feelings of persecution. [Segal, 1985, p. 25]

In other words, what is felt to be bad inside is put out or projected into the breast/mother/object and takes on the characteristics of a persecutor. A deep conviction emerges that others are not to be trusted and people are dangerous.

This extremity of human emotions becomes "split" in two important ways. First, there can be devaluation as well as idealization of this and future human relationships. When distrust is at its worst, infants, and later adults, can sometimes see others as "all good" or "all bad". We sometimes find ourselves at work, or in other social contexts, attributing excessive positive qualities to some individuals and, conversely, apparently intensely disliking others. It can be surprising that often we cannot quite explain why we harbour such feelings. At its most pathological, such splitting becomes the vehicle for part-object relationships where people are seen as numbers and "things" and a process of dehumanization has taken place. Of course, this can be the precursor of individual acts, murder or more collectively driven behaviours, and thought processes that happen at times of war or genocide. The powerful psychological process of putting all our badness in one person allows extreme violence to be justified. This is well described by a retired Second World War veteran who had been a US army officer in the South Pacific. One night the Japanese launched an infiltration attack on his position, during which a Japanese soldier charged him.

> I had my 45 [calibre pistol] in my hand ... And the point of the bayonet was no further than you are from me when I shot him. After everything had settled down, I helped search his body, you know, for intelligence purposes, and I found a photograph ... It was a picture of his wife, and these two beautiful children. Ever since, I've been haunted by the thought that these two beautiful children were growing up without their father, because I murdered their daddy. I'm not a young man any more and soon I'll have to answer to my maker for what I have done.

It is often the case in situations of war that national and international ideologies become idealized as way of justifying acts of inhumanity. Whether it is the creation of a pure Aryan race or the extermination of an evil empire, the individual soldier or terrorist believes they are killing to achieve a higher goal.

A second powerful operation of a splitting process is alluded to in Segal's earlier quote (see p. 18). Here, powerful, good and bad feelings are split off and put into/projected into the other person or social entity, who then becomes a "baddie" or persecutor. Alternatively, splitting off good feelings leads to the creation of "saints". Both polarities can be seen as a dysfunctional way of viewing the world and behaving towards others. In this model, then, human destructiveness is rooted in the failure of good experiences to win over bad experiences. These bad experiences become focused in negative feelings projected out on to others, leading to dehumanization and the potential for the further justification of hate and violence. Part of this violent process is also a deep emotional blueprint that relationships have to be conflictual and not cooperative. For Klein, this has its roots in each person's unconscious feeling about the act of parental intercourse and how they come into the world.

Good images of phantasies of parental intercourse bode well for healthy human relations. A positive view of coupling means that individuals feel there is a real possibility of relating together with harmony and affection. In psychoanalytic terminology, this is referred to as the resolution of the Oedipus Complex. For Freud, this involved a resolution of the rivalry between the child and their same sexed parent. However, Klein reconsidered these views and focused on the earlier infantile period of life (Anderson, 1992). For her, the fundamental image of parental intercourse dictates our human relations as we move into adulthood. Whatever perceptions and phantasies are formed about this relationship will affect the capacity to create good or bad object relations in later life. As Britton (1992) puts it:

> The perception of parental sexuality in the paranoid–schizoid position is phantastic and often horrific. It may form the basis of psychotic anxieties and perverse anxieties or crimes. One notable example is the phantasy of the combined parental figure. . . . In some patients the recognition of parental intercourse may be regarded as destructive of everything good about mother, or breast, and hence destructive of the good internal object which would be equated with everything good in the world. Thus, in such a patient the primal scene is likely to be seen as a catastrophe leading to a fallen world. As in the myth of the Garden of Eden, it is eating the

fruit of the tree of knowledge which brings the fall: the advent of shame and sex, and the avenging angel. [Britton, 1992, p. 42]

Thus, a perception of negative parental coupling can give rise to problems in creating fuller human relationships as we go through life; an internal opposition to emotional engagement persists. Bion describes this in terms of his own practice.

I have had occasions, in talking of the psychotic part of the person-ality, to speak of the destructive attacks which the patient makes on anything which is felt to have the function of linking one object to another. [Bion, 1957, p. 93]

Bion uses the term "psychotic part of the personality" to describe that element within us that has the propensity to attack and destroy either ourselves or others. This can take the form of emotional pres-sure or even physical violence.

The Kleinian model tends to view object relations in terms of these polarities, one of having the capacity to deal with ambiguities and developing the capacity to understand others and build rela-tionships; the other being a tendency to corrupt and destroy. Grin-berg (1975) has argued that we can subdivide the building of human relations into different spheres, according to four states of mind: L (love), H (hate), –K (against knowledge), and K (know-ledge). The first two states of mind are similar to what has been described earlier as idealization or devaluation, indicative of prim-itive splitting. The third state of mind is against any self-know-ledge, with the fourth state of mind describing the essence of the depressive position where learning from experiences takes place.

The final characteristic of the paranoid–schizoid position relates to the role of envy, the blame game, manic defences, and guilt. Joseph (1986) writes extensively on the envy that often exists in everyday life where, typically, the worth and creativity of others gets attacked and becomes denigrated. These subtle but everyday events have a cruel and destructive impact upon human relations.

Envy aims at being as good as the object, but, when this is felt as impossible, it aims at spoiling the goodness of the object, to remove the source of envious feelings. It is this spoiling aspect of envy that is so destructive to development. [Joseph, 1986, p. 40]

When people have embarked on a process of devaluation it is difficult to point to the source of this as envy. Often the destructive words and actions are so strong that the person, the object of the attack, cannot believe that this is a spoiling attack on their worthiness. This is where words can kill confidence. We can see this in our own lives, growing up, where children will remember "put downs" by adults and other children, rather than positive, constructive comments. These are easily internalized and become part of internal object relations that, in future, will tend to tear down rather than build up confidence. In the paranoid–schizoid position, where projection is seen as "normal", bad parts will be extensively located in the other.

An example of this occurred within a clinical setting with Raman Kapur, where the patient said, "I can't bear seeing good things in myself and others. When I see others flourishing I attack them with snide comments and smart remarks. I would use humour to humiliate, bring them down. That's the only way I can feel equal with others". Many people will often be the innocent recipients of these cruel and negative projections and believe that they are bad, whereas, instead, they have become the toilet for other people's inadequacy.

Envy can initiate projective processes so powerful that people's confidence and lives can be killed off. This hatred for the other quickly establishes a "blame game" culture of mutual projection. However, this can also become internal persecutory guilt, whereby the person blames themselves when relationships go wrong. This self-accusatory blame can have a masochistic flavour. This is difficult to correct unless the person develops concern for themselves and others, which can lead to a more reparative, instead of blaming, attitude. Somewhat paradoxically, the blame game at its most intense can lead to the development of false confidence spurred on by an appearance, however shallow, of superiority and contempt. This, Klein argued, leads to a series of manic defences where attributes of superior emotional cleanliness hides underlying envy or persecutory guilt.

As Segal puts it:

The manic relation to objects is characterised by a triad of feelings—control, triumph and contempt. These feelings are directly related to, and defensive against depressive feelings of valuing the object and depending on it and fear of loss and guilt. Control is a way of denying dependence, since an object that is wholly controlled is, up to a point, one that can be depended upon. Triumph is a denial of depressive feelings of valuing and caring; it is linked with omnipotence. . . . Contempt for the object is again a direct denial of valuing the object, which is so important in the depressive position, and it acts as a defence against the experience of loss and guilt. [Segal, 1973, pp. 83–84]

It is only when loss and guilt are experienced in terms of some understanding of the harm that is done to another person that repair can set in. This reparative urge is crucial for healthy human relations, from which constructive and valuable social interactions can take place. Unconsciously, this may be about repairing the damage done to objects earlier in one's life, but whatever its source it is the essence of creating a good society. To question and painfully reflect upon harm that has been done can be a route to the restoration of a more contented view about oneself and others; a position which can be distinguished from manic reparation, where there is a quick and superficial fix to make things better. Guilt and loss have to be experienced for true repair.

In this chapter we have briefly described some of the key concepts used by object relations theorists to build a model of explanation for the way people behave towards each other. It is useful at this point to describe and classify the types of thoughts, feelings and behaviours described by the paranoid–schizoid and depressive positions (see Table 1).

In summary, our mental health depends on whether we develop good or bad relationships with ourselves and others. In the model described earlier, and summarized in Table 1, it would be wrong to assume that we can simplistically place ourselves in one category or the other. It is more relatistic to understand the human experience in terms of shifts between the paranoid–schizoid and depressive positions (represented as P ⇔ D), depending on our state of human relations.

Destructive narcissism is another important characteristic of the paranoid–schizoid position. Holmes (2001) presents an overview of the concept of narcissism in both everyday life and clinical practice.

Table 1.

Paranoid–schizoid position	Depressive position
Paranoia/distrust	Trust and safety
Splitting into good and bad	Good and bad in everyone
Destructiveness	Creativity
Dysfunctional/hierarchical parental couple	Creative/equal parental couple
Envy	Pride in self and others
Attacks on links	Creation of links
Others are numbers, part of things	Concern for the fullness of other human beings
Hatred of reality	Acceptance of reality
Manic defence (control, triumph and contempt)	Relating thoughtfully with concern for self/others
Persecutory guilt	Reparative guilt
"Blame game"	Personal responsibility

In defining the concept he refers to relationships being like a hall of mirrors; we look to others as a source of validation. But this source of healthy validation of our own worth can move to a feeling associated more with destructiveness, where worth is gained out of devaluing and destroying others. Fundamental self-identity is gained from a position of triumph and superiority, which automatically, via the mechanism of projective identification, puts inadequate feelings into others. The person's soul is then cleansed and solidity and strength are gained from the excitement of adopting this "top-dog" position. As in the story of Black Narcissus, the destructive narcissistic, as with other types of narcissistic personalities, falls in love with his own image of himself, so creating a self-perpetuating idealization. In the story, Narcissus finds a pool of perfect water and stretches out to drink:

A strange new thirst, a craving, unfamiliar
Entered his body with the water
And entered his eyes

With the reflection in the limpid mirror
As the taste of water flooded him
So did love
                    [Hughes, 1997]

In falling deeply in love with his or her own image, a destructive narcissist becomes addicted to the taste of deathly acts from cruelty to murder.

Transference, counter-transference, projection and containment

It is important also to discuss briefly the importance of the concepts of transference and counter-transference in pychoanalytical theory. The term "transference" was first coined by Freud to describe how experiences from the past can be transferred on to the therapist. This occurs all the time and is normally referred to as people in authority becoming father or mother figures. Memories and experiences are then activated from the past and the person reacts to the authority figure as if they were the original parent. Emotional improvement and change occurs when people realize that these other figures will not react in a similar negative way through the "corrective emotional experience" of the new relationship. Melanie Klein took this further. She said that other people can represent parts of ourselves. So if we have a critical part of our personality, that becomes represented in the other person. Klein also placed particular emphasis on negative transferences and highlighted the importance of allowing these to develop. Change, in Klein's model, occurs through the person taking responsibility for the projections that are activated through the negative transference. In other words, "it's not them, it's me".

Counter-transference refers to the emotional reactions of the therapist. Again, there is a difference between Freud and Klein. Freud believed that all reactions in the therapist had to be analysed away; they were impediments to the therapeutic process. Conversely, Klein suggested that our reactions give us important clues as to what is happening in the other person. Our total reactions can be sensitive radar to let us know what is going on in the mind of the other person.

The concept of projection is crucial to Klein's model of human relationships. Projection is where we put *on to* others aspects of ourselves. So if we accuse someone of being arrogant, superior, or distant we may in fact be describing aspects of ourselves. The unthinkable thought is that "it could be me". Similarly, if we attribute to others positive characteristics such as intelligence, attractiveness, or knowledge, it may be that we are disowning aspects of ourselves that we can't bear. Change is about re-owning bad and good aspects of personality that we project into others. A further refinement of projection is called "projective identification". This is where we put our feelings *into* the other person without words. So we can leave people feeling sad, happy, and miserable by disowning our own feelings. Again, change is about re-owning projected parts of ourselves.

Finally, containment occurs when we are able to bear the emotions of others and return them to the sender in a benevolent and thoughtful way. Our usual way of responding to positive and negative projections is through either retaliation or collapse. A containing response detoxifies the negative elements of the projection/protective identification through our experience of maternal reverie (Bion, 1962). The proto-typical containing response may or may not have occurred in the early mother–infant relationship, where the messiness of the infant is transformed through the maternal, soothing, and calm response of the mother. The more toxic the projection the greater the transformational capacity required by the recipient.

An individual, group, or society exposed to human destructiveness will inevitably see paranoia, suspicion, and hate as normal. As Frankl said of the concentration camp, the "abnormal becomes normal". In this model of human relations, normal behaviour occurs where there are positive and constructive internal and external human relationships or object relations. To move from the paranoid–schizoid position requires a commitment to self-reflection and personal responsibility. It is only when we own what negative things we do to others that life can get better. Otherwise we are doomed to the transient pleasure of inflicting cruelty on ourselves and our fellow humans; we occupy the paranoid–schizoid position too frequently. These ideas are pursued, with particular reference to the Northern Ireland conflict, in the following chapters.

CHAPTER THREE

Object relations theory and the conflict in Northern Ireland

Introduction

So far we have outlined what we believe are key aspects of social and political life in Northern Ireland (Chapter One) and suggested psychoanalytical theory that may help us to understand aspects of this society (Chapter Two). We wish to emphasize that object relations theory offers one, albeit important, way of viewing some of the problematic individual, group, and societal problems of Northern Ireland. It cannot explain all such phenomena, of course; grand theories are very hard given the complexity of the late modern world in which we live. The volume of literature which focuses on the Northern Irish conflict simply confirms this sense of heterogeneity (Whyte, 1991). We also wish to emphasize that it is wrong to assume that all aspects of our individual and social life in Northern Ireland is necessarily troubled; of course there are a range of diverse experiences, good and bad, which are not easily described and analysed. Yet we feel it is important, in the following chapters, to develop a discussion about ways in which object relations theory might be applied to those situations that seem particularly problematic. Many of the social meanings and stereotypes that contribute to negative human relations in the context of the Troubles can be viewed as pathological in that they are often constructed from perceptions driven by anxiety, paranoid states, and collective failure to see "the good with the bad". It may be that the pressure to maintain and reproduce dysfunctional and maladaptive patterns of object relationships in Northern Ireland is extremely forceful. The punitive superego, whether it is the external political object or the internal object, promises terror and persecution if it is not obeyed.

Group and social processes: connecting the individual with the structural

Although a causal relationship between individual thought processes and broader social processes is difficult to establish, we now want to suggest that a tentative exploration of their applicablity in Northern Ireland may be worthwhile. It is useful to note that other writers have sought to make connections between the inner world of the pyche and social conflict, although in other contexts. For example, Michael Rustin, someone who has applied Kleinian theory to social processes within British society, suggests important relationships between individual and social spheres:

> The idea of development and fulfillment of the person through relationship, both internal and external, which is implicit in this [Kleinian] psychoanalytic account, is a distinctively "social" one. I want to stress this point—it might seem obvious—because it goes against the widespread idea that society will be better when and if we merely give more opportunity and goods to the "individual". It is the quality of relationships that individuals can generally have with others around them—and we must include phantasised and symbolic others—which make for contentment and activity, not merely gratifications of various kinds. The most beautiful house with a swimming pool is obtained at a serious psychic price when there has to be an armed man at the gate to keep out intruders. [Rustin, 1991, pp. 47–48]

What might be described as "armed states of mind" bring a pseudo-contentment for some people in Northern Ireland. We seem to be aware, for example, that individuals and groups experience the Troubles differently. Thus middle-class professionals, like the two authors of this book, live in quite well to-do areas which, in some ways, have been insulated from the violence faced by people living in more deprived districts. Many members of the middle classes have built swimming pools "out of sight and out of mind" of troubled areas of Northern Ireland, hoping material contentment would bring them peace of mind. Some of these concepts have also been operationalized to explain the psychodynamic process in play at times of national and international conflict. Segal describes the way in which functioning in the paranoid–schizoid position can lead to projective processes in large groups. She writes:

> Group function is often basically influenced and disrupted by psychotic phenomena. Freud said that we form groups for two reasons: one to "combat the forces of nature"; and the other to bind "man's destructiveness to man". Groups typically deal with this destructiveness by splitting, the group itself being idealised and held together by brotherly love, and collective love of the ideal, whilst destructiveness is directed outwards to other groups. [Segal, 1995, p. 194]

At other levels of group identity and process, division and destructive intent is commonplace. Rosenfeld (1987) and Steiner (1993) have written about the internal psychic organization in severely disturbed people who seem to "get a kick" out of being hurtful to others and where a dedication to destructiveness prevents opportunities for the development of more positive relationships with others. The self-esteem gained from such internal processes led to Rosenfeld coining the phrase "destructive narcissism".

> The destructive narcissitic parts of the self are linked to a psychotic structure or organisation which is split off from the rest of the personality. This psychotic structure is like a delusional world or object, into which parts of the self tend to withdraw. It appears to be dominated by an omnipotent or omniscient, extremely ruthless part of the self, which creates the notion that within the delusional object there is complete painlessness and also the freedom to indulge in any sadistic activity. The whole structure is committed to narcissistic self-sufficiency and is strictly directed against any object-relatedness. [Rosenfeld,1987, p. 112]

There is a sense in which members of many political, social, and paramilitary groups in Northern Ireland often appear to have idealized destructiveness, almost incorporating and encouraging aggressiveness in imagery and discourse. There is a vernacular phrase the "hard man" which is used in our society to describe this type of personality. Refusal to speak and work with others symbolizes an idealization of self-sufficiency that is contained within a hard-man approach to the world. Destructive narcissism entails bullying and a capacity for the contemptuous put down, which are recognized as legitimate. Hard words and thoughts build towards an habitual form of day-to-day verbal terrorism that brings its own "feel good factors". A quote from Ian Paisley highlights this: "I am anti-Roman Catholic, but, God being my Judge, I love the poor dupes who are ground down under that system" (quoted by Deutsch & McGowan, 1973). The harshness of this mindset becomes most pronounced in the discourses of the many paramilitary groups which emerged during the thirty years of the conflict. Here are a few examples. Eamon Collins, a former member of the IRA who was allegedly murdered by the same organization, talked about his feelings when "promoted" to become an interrogator and assassin:

> My promotion to the security unit had given me an initial glow of satisfaction. I tried to allow the swelling of my ego to overshadow the horror of what I was involved in. [Collins, 1997, p. 232]

The displacement of morality and concern for human values by destructive narcissism is also evident in the following extract from a book by Michael Stone, a loyalist terrorist:

> Herron handed me the Webley [gun] and the Bible. I swore on the open Bible to be a faithful and honourable member of the Ulster Defence Association. I swore to defend my community. I promised to be a guardian of my people and to fight to protect them with every drop of my loyalist blood. The service was over in minutes. I felt good. I was on a high. I was swept away by the romanticism of it all. It didn't enter my head that I had just committed myself to a life of violence. I was in love with the idea of being the great defender, the knight in shining armour looking after my people. [Stone, 2003, p. 32]

Ulster rage

The destructive impulse projected outwards is first experienced as oral aggression. I believe that oral–sadistic impulses towards the mother's breast are active from the beginning of life, though with the onset of teething the cannibalistic impulses increase in strength—a factor stressed by Abraham. [Klein (1946), reprinted in Mitchell, 1986, p. 180]

The rage experienced in Northern Ireland has the quality of an infant at a mother's breast. Biting, attacking, cannibalistic "tearing people" to pieces is often acted out in everyday life with disastrous consequences. In object relations theory, poor maternal containment in early life leads to residual aggressive impulses being omnipresent in everyday human relations. Evacuation of aggressive feelings fulfils the goal of sadism of providing temporary measure, but unfortunately does not provide the quality of containment that substitutes aggression for more purposeful and creative activities. This is aptly described by the Israeli military psychologist, Ben Shalit.

On my right was mounted a heavy machine gun. The gunner (normally the cook) was firing away with what I can only describe as a beatific smile on his face. He was exhilarated by the squeezing of the trigger, the hammering of the gun and the flight of his tracers ... into the dark shore. It struck me then (and was confirmed by him and many others later) that squeezing the trigger—releasing a hail of bullets—gives enormous pleasure and satisfaction. There are the pleasures of combat, not in terms of the intellectual planning—of the tactical and strategic chess game—but of the primal aggression, the release and the orgasmic discharge. [quoted in Grossman, 1996, p. 136]

Here, Shalit is clearly linking killing with sexual satisfaction. In Kleinian terminology, the death instinct has got mixed up with the life instinct. Pleasure is not gained from constructive or creative experiences, it is gained from the destructiveness inflicted on others. This is a common phenomenon noticed by many psychoanalysts in work with psychotic patients (Rosenfeld, 1987). Whether it is loathing or destructive verbal acts, pleasure is gained from the murder of body or soul. This, theoretically, would suggest that no modification or switch in the death instinct has occurred towards more pleasurable or creative experiences. It may be, however, that in the peace process we are beginning to see the signs of this creative impulse. Northern Ireland is beginning to see regeneration schemes and new cultural and art developments taking place. Possibly there is now a window of opportunity for depressive position functioning, where pride is taken in the construction of good things rather than in human destruction. Again, Eamon Collins refers to this wish to change the mind to focus on more human endeavours.

> The constant pressure seeped gradually, like a poison jag, into every corner of my mind. I had come to ditch almost everything and everybody not connected in some way to the IRA. It had become my whole life and I was beginning to ask myself what sort of life I had. I went through the motions of enjoying myself, but how could I live happily when I spent most of my time in the company of people whose business was death? And I was one of them. Always looking for people to kill, finding people to do the killing, constantly exposing myself to danger, more and more danger. [Collins, 1997, pp. 158–159]

There are many statistics to indicate that "Ulster rage" may be "alive and unwell" in day-to-day life. Those of particular relevance are listed below.

- Although deaths from coronary heart disease have been falling since the early 1980s, Northern Ireland still has one of the highest death rates in Europe.
- Road traffic collisions are a major cause of death and serious injury. Every year around 200 people are killed, more than 1,500 are seriously injured, and over 11,000 receive slight injuries. Northern Ireland has a worse road safety record for child fatalities than most other European countries. Furthermore, the government, through the Department of Health and Social Services and Public Safety, states that most road deaths or serious injuries are avoidable. The main cause remains excessive speed.
- Breastfeeding rates in Northern Ireland are one of the lowest in Europe. Initial breastfeeding rates in 2000 were 71% in England and Wales; 63% in Scotland and 54% in Northern

Ireland. Although still low, this represents a significant rise from a 1995 figure of 45%.

• Northern Ireland has the highest level of professional soccer fouls in the UK.

Could it be that "Ulster rage" is being "acted out" through many Type A personalities, who are most susceptible to coronary heart disease? These personalities are strict, harsh, and aggressive in their treatment of themselves and others, with research documenting the link between this personality type and heart disease. In contrast, a softer, relaxed, and affectionate "Type B" personality is less suscep- tible to heart disease. Could it also be that we "act out" our aggres- sion on the road? More and more research is linking life-style to road traffic accidents. It may be that we have so much unprocessed "Ulster rage" in Northern Ireland from the effects of the Troubles that we express this through car rage. Could it be also that the lack of breastfeeding has led to a lack of maternal containment in the mother–child relationship? If we take seriously the Kleinian idea that maternal containment is important in soothing the aggressive impulses of babies, then it may be that the lack of breastfeeding leads to a great deal of primitive aggression. It is important to note that when Klein suggests this theory it is not crucial that it is breast rather than bottle feeding. The process of soothing, irrespective of the actual soothing object itself, is the critical ingredient in lessening rage. Finally, could it also be that in sport we act out our aggression by "kicking the hell" out of our opponents?

All of these hypotheses are offered as food for thought. We cannot ignore the effect of exposing human beings to destructive experiences. If we have an idea that rage remains unprocessed we may then take responsibility as adults to ensure we do not repeat experiences that only worsen the rageful states of mind that are being carried about from day to day.

Object relations theory can help in our understanding of violence in this society through the use of concepts of persecutory anxiety, harsh and critical superegos and aggression fuelled by paranoia. Menzies Lyth's (1988) discussion of how early primitive object rela- tions manifest themselves in aberrant car driving may make sense in the Northern Ireland context where deaths through road traffic acci- dents are well above the UK average. She suggests that unresolved infantile rage becomes channelled aggressively because of the poor maternal containment plus the failure to create a benevolent societal atmosphere. Local politicians have rarely moved beyond entrenched, paranoid perspectives, and the continued existence of a British administration that denies responsibility for its part in the conflict has led to what has been called the "democratic deficit", with no visible opportunity for political containment of the conflict.

Paranoia and aggression are intimately linked where suspiciousness will lead to the patient feeling that they are about to be attacked. A prevailing paranoid atmosphere, as in the recent Drumcree incident, where marchers from the Orange Order felt outraged that the Catholic community objected to their "traditional route" of walking down a particular road, creates an environment where people feel they are about to be attacked and are willing to defend themselves at all costs from this real or imagined threat.

Our thesis is that Northern Ireland society has been so damaged by its violent history that everyday relationships are inevitably contaminated by mistrust; new experiences are not welcomed as opportunities to achieve richer human relationships, but are perceived rather as the possible erosion and decline of the individual in society. For this society to change, good experiences must prevail and be genuinely offered as an alternative to bad experiences, so that individuals can form a greater trust of others. In Kleinian theory, individual psychopathology is manifested through the fear of destructive impulses destroying either valued internal or external experiences. The individual in the paranoid–schizoid position finds him or herself dominated by thoughts and feelings of wishing to damage those that are valued. Essentially, these are activated by an awareness of dependence that is deeply hated by the paranoid–schizoid or "psychotic" part of the personality. For this part of the personality, mutual dependence characterized by intimacy and generosity are unbearable as feelings, and omnipotence and omniscience become the valued ways of relating. The term "manic defence" is used to describe the denial of the reality of humans needing each other for growth and development. Segal writes:

> The intensity of pain and anxiety in the depressive position mobilises new and powerful defences, namely the system of manic defences. The manic defences involve regression to splitting, denial, idealisation and projection, basically schizoid mechanisms, but

organised into a system to protect the ego from the experience of depressive anxiety. The depressive anxiety arises out of the infant's recognition of the mother as a whole object on whom he depends and in relation to whom he experiences ambivalence and the consequent guilt and fear of loss. Because of this, the whole relation has to be denied. Denial of the importance of his object and triumph over it, control, contempt and devaluation take the place of depressive feelings. [Segal, 1981/1985, pp. 14–15]

As with the concept of the "hard man" described in Chapter Four, the fundamental blueprint of these forms of human relations is a violent intercourse between two objects. Thus, relationships become dangerous and can only be dealt with by distance and paranoia. The manic pace of everyday life perversely ensures that intimacy and dependency are minimized. Conflict and tension, which emerge from "manic" relatedness, can lead to the establishment of a normal way of relating which values distance. Perversely, this can also lead to an "addiction to sadism" (Joseph, 1982), whereby pleasure is gained from aggressive human relations. This perversion of pleasure is most clearly seen in working with the sexual offending behaviour of adults (Meltzer, 1973), and in a much milder form may manifest itself in a society over-exposed to violence. This addiction can lead to a feeling of fullness and potency, so justifying the interest taken in participating in violent relationships. Unfortunately, the end result is a personality predisposed to emotional detachment, where attack is the best form of defence, it is better to be in control, to trust no one, and know your enemy.

In Northern Irish society these personality traits can be found at the interpersonal level, where excessively critical and inflexible judgements are made of others, often with little rational justification. The language and symbolism of culture becomes the mechanism to antagonise and humiliate "the other"—for example in the traditional slogans of "Brits Out" and "No Surrender". An interesting variation on this theme has been the use of the Irish language by some parts of the Republican movement to both reinforce their community identity as well as limit purposeful discourse with "the other". Some members of the Unionist community have responded by appealing for the recognition of Ulster-Scots as a language by the state. The use of language to reinforce cultural identity is a double-edged sword; it can be a genuine attempt to celebrate diversity and share mutually beneficial traditions or can be used to exclude "the other" and limit the possibility for conflict resolution. In this culture of manic defences the idea of "good enough" or "more good than bad" is rarely accepted. Instead, a cult of perfectionism or exclusivism is desired. In Northern Ireland there is, for example, a high premium placed on academic rather than emotional intelligence (Goleman, 1996) or "common sense wisdom". This splitting process is reflected in the way that the educational system functions. On the one hand, Northern Ireland's education records boast some of the highest academic results, but on the other, the highest levels in the UK of children leaving school with no qualifications.

These harsh, confrontational ways of thinking and behaviour occur at other levels of society. For example, in a recent confrontation, prior to the symbolic Twelfth of July parades, the Reverend Ian Paisley warned "We will die if necessary rather than surrender" (*The Independent*, 12 July 1995). Just as there are symbols of intransigence and no surrender in Northern Irish society, so to there is evidence of manic defence and a willingness to triumph over "the other" in everyday lives.

For these reasons change may be limited, but is none the less possible. There is evidence in Northern Ireland that hope and cautious optimism exist despite the traumas of the past thirty years. The current ceasefire, preceded by the emergence of cross-community dialogue culminating in the Good Friday Agreement (Northern Ireland Office (NIO), 1998a), suggests that this society has the propensity for productive and healthy change. In the past decade, the development of three separate centres for psychoanalytic psychotherapy is having a significant impact on teaching and training for professionals and care for people with mental health problems (Ekins, 1991; Kapur *et al.*, 1997). These developments offer hope that a society will emerge in which more tolerant perceptions of the other will prevail.

No surrender

"No Surrender" and "Belfast Says No" campaigns have characterized the state of mind of many people in Northern Ireland towards a style of relatedness that leads to violence. There is strength to be gained from maintaining a non-compliant position, even if this results, directly or indirectly, in human destructiveness. Pride, stubbornness, and resistance to change, even if this change improves the quality of life of people saying "No", highlights a link to the dependence on other people. If people say "Yes", they have to open themselves up to dialogue and negotiation, which brings its own vulnerabilities. Depending on others opens up new possibilities but also brings new vulnerabilities. A well-known psychoanalyst, Herbert Rosenfeld, makes a similar observation in his work with disturbed and difficult states of mind.

> In the last ten years I have made further detailed observations and have changed my views in so far as I believe that some deadly force inside the patient, resembling Freud's description of the death instinct, exists and can be clinically observed. In some patients this destructive force manifests itself as a chronic paralysing resistance which can hold up analysis for many years. In others, it takes the form of a deadly but hidden force which keeps the patient away from living and occasionally causes severe anxieties about being overwhelmed and killed. It is this deadly force which resembles most closely Freud's description of a death instinct that remains mute and hidden but opposes the patient's desire to live and to get better. [Rosenfeld, 1987, p. 107]

Could it be that in Northern Ireland we have become so fixated with deadly forces that there is an inherent opposition to a better life? Unconsciously, and out of the awareness of everyday life, the "No" position can act as a source of self-esteem, giving a feel-good factor and a sense of pride that the right thing is being done, yet destructiveness continues. Within this paranoid–schizoid position, experiences with others are unbearable, and if human contact is aroused, dependency becomes a real issue. Michael Stone describes this ritualized state of mind:

> In my paramilitary life, I had a ritual. I never looked at newspapers and I never watched television reports. The radio was my only source of news. Mid morning bulletins confirmed Patrick Brady's death [someone he had killed] and that same day the UFF claimed responsibility for the murder in a telephone call to Downtown

Radio. I tried to look at Brady's death in a detached way. He was a soldier [a member of Sinn Fein] and I was a soldier, and in war, soldiers die. I didn't want to expose myself to the human aspect, the grieving widow and the weeping children, because that's when it becomes real. This is when a target becomes a human being. The grief and pain of the target's loved ones would be enough to make me stop. I wasn't a trophy loyalist, unlike many of my colleagues. I tried to look at it as a job that had to be done. I tried to see the target as a target, not a human being, but when I pulled the trigger a little part of me died too. I tried not to feel anything but I did. Only a monster would feel nothing. When you take a man's life you lose part of yourself and part of your humanity forever. [Stone, 2003, pp. 71–72]

Saying no externally also acts as a way of saying no internally to feelings and thoughts associated with destructive acts. Idealization of the "No" state of mind brings with it a justification embedded in a moralization of acts. It was done because "it was the right thing to do". Any movement from "No" is seen as a weakness. Yet, as in the peace process, it is potentially a source of strength in bringing with it constructive and creative acts. But can people change their minds? The current stage of the peace process demonstrates that this is possible if people give up, albeit begrudingly, the negative state of mind that is the source of so much destructiveness. This melting of the "No Surrender" position is highlighted in the biography of David Ervine (Sinnerton, 2002), a leading loyalist and now leader of the Progressive Unionist Party. During his time in prison, he met Gusty Spence, a well-known loyalist terrorist who had, by his own admission, murdered Catholics. In prison, both made use of education facilities which were made available by the then Chief Probation Officer, Mrs Breidge Gadd (now chairperson of the mental health charity, Threshold). This meant that human encounters took place between Catholic and Protestant prisoners, which created an opportunity for the lessening of an "Ulster says No" position. Sinnerton (2002) writes of this humanization process:

What was it like when these bitter enemies, the personification of all the hatred and brutality of their warring communities, met face to face? When a Loyalist met a Republican for the first time, suspicion and distrust soured the air initially, but he discovered eventually they had things in common, as Martin Snodden [Loyalist prisoner] described:

When I started going to the study huts, I had by chance chosen a room and an Official IRA man had chosen the same room. So we're in the same room and we got talking. I can remember him making me tea and me thinking "I wonder is he putting anything into that tea". And I'm sure he was thinking the same when it was my turn. Whenever we had tea breaks, we would have been chatting and we were saying where we came from and why we had ended up there, with the realisation that we had a lot in common and had almost been hoodwinked into being involved in the conflict, and the irresponsibility of the so-called leadership in the country. Not just politicians, but so-called prominent people in the country. [Sinnerton, 2002, p. 64]

And David Ervine adds, on the humanization process,

We had a relationship [with the IRA] that was cordial and respectful. I think there may have been a couple of friendships that grew out of it. But we were us and they were them. Maybe we proved something: that "them and us" can actually cohabit, that "them and us" can get on, that "them and us" without losing one ounce of principle, can function together. That was important. Another lesson learned. And remember, these guys came from Catholic backgrounds. They came from Catholic, working class areas. They came from sectarianism as did me in many ways, and yet we learned the capacity to cope with each other and they only had one head, two arms and two legs, just like me! [Sinnerton, 2002, p. 66]

In Kleinian terminology, part-object relationships were moving to whole-object relationships with the associated capacity for concern developing in a mutually dependent and reciprocal relationship. This "Ulster says Yes" process has provided an opportunity for peace that we all must take.

Ulster fry

For the rest of the day none of the interrogators let up the pressure. They kept pushing and pulling my chair, telling me to sit up as I was too uncomfortable. In a later session with the first pair who had interviewed me, the younger cop of the team spent a long time detailing the injuries to civilians as a result of the mortar attack. During all of these interrogations, whenever one of the interrogators spoke directly to me, the other one would leave the room, ostensibly to get a cup of tea. But they would always return after a few minutes and begin their own direct questioning, following logically from what had just gone on before. I was sure that when they left the room they would spend time looking through the spy hole to observe my body language more closely. . . . I had survived two days of interrogation. On Sunday, during the second interrogation before lunch, I found myself once again with the first pair of interrogators. They were even angrier than before. The younger man spoke through clenched teeth when he was not shouting directly into my ear. He said "I'm going to the first of many funerals today. After the funerals I'm going to your house and we are going to turn it upside down. I'm going to arrest your wife and she's coming here for seven days . . ." "Your wife, I'm booked in to see her for the first interview, then after that I'm coming straight round to see you". I could feel his breath on my face. "And you know, Eamon, I've got a name for your wife. I'm not going to call her Bernadette . . . If they had taken me out of the interrogation room and brought me to a room where they would have shown me my wife, I would have broken. [Collins, 1997, pp. 266–267]

An "Ulster fry" is a well known regional breakfast in Northern Ireland. High in fat but also high in filling up bellies with a "good feed". The sizzling of the sausages, bacon, eggs, black pudding, potato, and soda bread is similar to the sizzling of human minds that takes place in the troubled mind of Northern Ireland. Here, as highlighted through the interrogative experiences above, pride is taken in being able to "grill" people with cruelty and sadism. Justification can always be found for being cruel to others. But in Northern Ireland we have grown up with cruelty being normal and compassion abnormal. A well-known psychoanalyst, Eric Brenman, writes about the mechanisms of cruelty and narrow-mindedness:

In normal development love modifies cruelty; in order to perpetuate cruelty, steps have to be taken to prevent human love from operating. My contention is that in order to maintain the practice of cruelty, a singular narrow-mindedness of purpose is put into operation. This has the function of squeezing out humanity and preventing human understanding from modifying the cruelty. The consequence of this process produces a cruelty which is inhuman. [Brenman, reprinted in 1995, p. 256)

To be cruel you have to cut out humanity from yourself and the other person in order to be able to cut them to pieces. In the interrogation example, the cruelty of the terrorist attack by Collins, where people were killed by mortars, was accompanied by the cruelty of the police officers interrogating a human being. Here, as stated earlier, the powerful processes of justification and moralization are activated to execute a cruel act. Cruelty is delivered as a way of "doing what is right for others".

This form of cruelty inevitably finds its way into helping and caring relationships in this society. For example, following the publication of an article on helping professionals in the aftermath of the Omagh bombing (Kapur, 2001), the author was met with particularly cruel accusations of "acting as a vulture", sucking on the blood of victims to boost my own self-esteem. This experience "in the transference" is also aptly described by the clinical example that Brenman gives in his treatment of a Jewish patient who constantly derided him and whose family was a victim of Nazi concentration camps. His experience of this counter-transference is as follows:

> Gradually I was able to study the dossier she has built up about me. I was depicted as complacent and smug, and she seemed determined to put an end to my peace of mind. She maintained that I practised analysis solely in order to make money and in order to believe I knew everything about life. She tried to make me feel that my whole belief in psychoanalysis was based on a lie, motivated by my greedy omniscience. Above all, she wanted to know if I could face this false life I had built up; face the illusion and the guilt and have to give it up with nothing to fall back on. She even begrudged the fact I could practise as a doctor if I realised psychoanalysis was a delusion; I was to be left with nothing at all. . . . These attacks on me were her attempt to destroy my goodness and creativity. [Brenman, 1995, p. 259]

These experiences occur regularly in day-to-day interactions in the troubled mind of Northern Ireland. Generosity and creativity are attacked, perverted, and negatively transformed into actions aimed at destroying the confidence of others. For the person offering creativity and generosity, their position often becomes unbearable as there is a tremendous pressure to act out negative feelings, so confirming to the world that life is a cruel place after all. Generating and sustaining good experiences in a paranoid–schizoid world is extremely difficult.

Two mechanisms keep cruelty alive. One is narrow-mindedness, where a person cannot think about, feel, or see the other person as a full human being. There is more to the person than meets the narrowness of the eye. In Kleinian theory, this again would be linked to the early mother–infant relationship where the baby sees only the nipple, not the breast, mother, and the whole person who will have feelings if her nipple is attacked. Similarly, in human relationships of cruelty, people are not seen, only mechanical and dehumanized parts of them. In addition, omnipotence is rife. Cruelty is delivered on behalf of achieving some truth or omnipotently to make a "wrong right". This moral position is felt to be superior to human love and forgiveness. The only way out of this paranoid–schizoid state of mind is for us all to invest in understanding, see the bigger picture, and realize that human beings are always involved in conflict.

As we were writing this book the Hutton Enquiry was taking place. Chaired by Lord Hutton, a judge from Northern Ireland, the enquiry was a quest for the truth. But we had someone who was bred in the troubled mind of Northern Ireland sitting in judgement on the government of the day. We also saw that Dr Kelly took his own life as an act of cruelty to himself that reflected the cruelty he felt was inflicted on him, particularly through the public "grilling" he suffered. The question for British society is whether Hutton's form of an "Ulster Fry" got to the truth or served only to further hide another possibility: that British political minds got hijacked into a narrow-minded analysis which not only led to the death of Dr Kelly, but to that of many others. There is, after all, no understanding and compassion with an "Ulster Fry".

CHAPTER FOUR

Working with individuals affected by the Troubles

T rouble leads to trouble and violence breeds violence. This is an unmistakable truth of human relationships. When we have an opportunity to study a troubled or traumatized state of mind on the couch, we see in minute detail the effects of human destructiveness.

In psychoanalytic practice this is the traditional method of observing emotional life. In this chapter we use the concepts of transference, counter-transference, projection, and containment to describe clinical phenomena seen on the couch that highlight the results of a human mind exposed to violence.

Troubled transferences

A new patient entered the room for the first time and took the couch.

> *Patient*: I don't know what to do here. [Silence.] I'm feeling all at sea. [Silence.] Why don't you say anything, tell me what to do. Maybe I'm wasting my time coming to see you. I don't seem to get any answers. [Silence.] OK, so maybe I'll begin to talk if you don't say anything.

In this first session general things were happening:

- the patient immediately felt I was cruel and abandoning
- he also felt I was no good to him because I did not immediately become the expert
- he finally takes responsibility for talking.

In those early moments I was being seen as a distant, uncaring, authority figure who knew very little. Allowing the relationship to unfold highlights the views the patient has of others. In my experience of working with individuals in Northern Ireland, other, more troubled, transferences have appeared.

Drumcree transference

The experience of being dominated and oppressed by the other side is both real and imagined in Northern Ireland. Imagined take-overs or transferences are rooted in fundamentally bad experiences in both the Catholic and Protestant traditions. Examples of both illustrate the reality of what has taken place, which sets up the deep fear that people will be trodden upon—what I call the "Drumcree transference".

Eamon Collins, a member of the IRA for many years, writes:

Even before Unionism bared its teeth in the Civil Rights movement's face in 1969, I knew there was something amiss in the State into which I had been born. .... As a young person growing up I began to witness the historical conflicts described by my mother being lured out, and saw them through her eyes. I remember in 1968 returning from the seaside and my parents pulling into a layby to listen to news bulletins about a man shot dead in Armagh by B Specials. I knew only Protestants could be B Specials ... The "B-men" were our neighbours. They were armed; we were not. The significance of this, coupled with memories of historical disempowerment of Catholics, began to seem very urgent. I was looking at the organisation that was beating Catholics daily on protest marches. Comrades of these very people who were shooting Catholics dead. Fear and excitement mingled even more intensely in my mind. [Collins, 1997, p. 41]

An alternative analysis of the motivations of becoming a para-military terrorist is outlined by David Ervine, a member of the loyalist UVF for many years.

I was sitting in what was called Clancys Tavern, at the corner of Albertbridge Road and Castlereagh Street. There was a ground-floor bar, a middle lounge and a top lounge. I was in the top lounge and I could see the puffs of smoke go off in Belfast. I think that was the beginning of the end. It was so brutal, so raw. The best means of defence is attack. Maybe that sounds simplistic but that's how I felt. [Sinnerton, 2002, p. 30]

Both people felt convinced that the only way to end oppression and prevent dominance was by violence. There is an arguable real-ity to both these claims. The cartoon from the *Guardian* in 1996 aptly illustrates this reality (Figure 2). However, the presence of so much dominance in Northern Ireland society has led to people imagining that there will be dominance when there may not be—a transfer-ence reaction.

Clinically, the fear of being taken over and dominated by the other side is illustrated by the following account taken from a

Figure 2. Steve Bell cartoon, the *Guardian*, 12 July 1996.

patient I saw in 1996 when the first Drumcree march was pushed through.

> It's those bloody Protestants, they think they can take over and march over all us Catholics, who the hell do they think they are. If I had my way I'd ship them out of the country . . . those Protestants feel they can take over the country.

Whether real or imagined, people in Northern Ireland live in fear from day to day of being taken over by the other side. In this transference the patient clearly felt I was going to dominate the vulnerable parts of him. Of course, this will happen in many situations. However, if we react as if we feel this will always occur, we are creating a self-fulfilling prophecy. The task of the receiver of a negative transference is *not* to fulfil the phantasy of the other. This is the only way to develop more constructive human relations and, most of all, the patience to make sure bullying roles are not acted out.

Bully transference

This idealization of aggression has been described elsewhere (Kapur & Campbell, 2002) where an example is taken from everyday psychoanalytic practice to illustrate the preponderance of this negative state of mind. In this clinical example a single 40-year-old patient entered psychotherapy with extreme suspicion and distrust of my (RK's) motives in offering help. His manner was stiff and controlled and he would take the couch in a very regimented manner, as if he were participating in a military routine. I could feel his aggression, via projective identification, particularly at the start of sessions, where he wanted to stamp his authority. In the early stages of the psychotherapy the atmosphere would be characterized by a mixture of hostility and intimidating silence. In these sessions I felt anxious about being too accurate with my interpretations for fear of being called a "smart bastard" and also equally worried about being incorrect and open to accusations of being insensitive and stupid. The imminence of these attacks felt very real and I felt the superior "Lordness" of the power towering over me when I greeted him at the door (he was taller than I). This patient terminated psychotherapy after a session when he freely associated about the murder of Rajeev Gandhi in India. When I interpreted his wishes to murder me, he protested vehemently, complaining I was "way off the mark". It may have been that I was too accurate, or generally he felt the psychotherapy was going nowhere that caused him to decide to terminate the sessions. He returned several months later, complaining that the difficulties that originally prompted him to seek help had not diminished. Inevitably, the presence of the "hard man" had left him suffering from these internal attacks. The existence of such harshness, accompanied with intense persecution and suspicion, is consistent with a harsh and severe punitive superego.

What this case illustrates is the way in which the violent world outside permeates the internal world of the patient and the helping relationship. The therapist, in the mind of the patient, became the enemy on the other side of the sectarian divide in Northern Ireland. The cultural context becomes embedded in therapeutic interchange. This patient worried that I would "plant a bomb" in his mind and blow him to pieces; that I would terrorize him with my interventions and, with no prior "telephone warnings" damage him either through anticipated verbal attacks or with no planning in breaks. In Northern Ireland, telephone warnings precede bombs exploding. This analogy was pursued in the ongoing psychotherapy. In relation to breaks, when I suggested that these might indeed be traumatic, the patient could not decide whether this was an attempt at deception, intended to play havoc with his internal life, or a genuine attempt to work through separation and feelings of abandonment. This patient would also highlight the importance of "attacking before being attacked". Psychic violence seemed inevitable and his defence against this was to deliver the first blow. His mind, like the society he was living in, was subject to warnings of constant violence, so he had to be externally alert to the possibility of being attacked. His internal security forces had to patrol his external relationships in case he would be ambushed or boobytrapped by the therapist's interpretations.

When a society is exposed to so much violence the bully is always seen as the winner. Hitting others with great force is seen as delivering the ultimate knock-out blow. In this domineering dialogue there is little room for calm, thoughtful reflection and considered debate. This may lead to the person not having an outcome they want, which would be seen as a weakness to the psychotic personality. This is described by a patient who said:

> My mind holds out an idea with fierce loyalty that life is about going for it in a big way with all guns blazing and really, basically, relentlessly going after the big one type of thing and that is what life is all about.

Dominance is the name of the game; someone has to be top dog and it's got to be him. This domineering instinct is part and parcel of a mind exposed to troubled relationships. The psychotic personality, which values destructiveness over creativity, is activated. Hate dominates over love. Relationships occur at a superficial level with little concern for others. Triumph over others is seen as the ultimate goal. In Northern Ireland we see this troubled mind factor in many situations:

- politicians who shout the loudest and who are the masters of "put-down" get all the attention;
- civic leaders who ridicule and humiliate get into the headlines;
- killer "emotional punches" become the way to do business.

Within Northern Ireland we see tremendous primitive splits. This societal fracture is best highlighted through the idealization of academic and professional positions and the devaluation of everything else. The bully has the brains and everyone else is stupid.

When this bullying transference is so intense, the pressure to re-enact a bullying and aggressive response is massive. To do otherwise is seen as a weakness. But the only way to move to a depressive position is to realize that the bully is acting out of a fear of failure and their own inadequacy. This may stop the vicious psychotic cycle, thus preventing the ultimate destructive act; that of murdering someone else because you feel that otherwise they will dominate you.

The cartoon illustrating the continuation of the empire bully points to the idealization of top dog aggression in the Unionist psyche (Figure 3). This is part of day-to-day discourse in Northern Ireland and is activated by many events. Eamon Collins describes this activation of primitive aggression.

Undefeated Champion
of the
British Empire
1922—1938

Figure 3.   Cartoon depicting "the empire bully": Stewart, *PTQ*, Belfast 1938.

My mother left school after the war to work as a hairdresser in
Belfast, where she experienced petty-minded discrimination by
Protestants. This experience drove her home to Crossmaglen to
work in her father's grocery shop, which had begun to prosper.
The family business expanded into ice-cream manufacture and
they bought a van to take to public events across the North. One
of her brothers, Frank, had a particular keen eye for money making
opportunities; he decided once to drive the van to a big Orange-
man's parade at Rathfriland, around thirty miles from Crossmaglen.
Frank knew that the name emblazoned on the family van "John
Cumiskey and Sons, Crossmaglen" would identify the occupants as
Catholics from an idea known to be disloyal to the state. But he had
been reared on stories of how his father had sold apples and oranges

to Protestants at dances and so he was prepared to take a chance, believing that the Orangemen's appetite for ice-cream would be stronger than their appetite for Fenian blood . . . my mother . . . felt a little anxious as she set off in the ice-cream van at the height of the marching season, knowing that the month of July had become a time when most of her fellow Catholics tried to keep out of sight . . . but as the day turned to evening she grew frightened, the sound of drums seeming to drive the Orangemen into a frenzy of aggression . . . a tall, dark-haired man wearing a suit, bowler hat and orange sash tried to pull open the side door while screaming obscenities; "Fucking papists from Crossmaglen . . . he was joined in his efforts by several other men, all smelling of drink . . . They rocked the vehicle to and fro, their engaged flushed faces mouthing anti-Catholic invective, "Fenian bitch, Romish cunt". Frank she told me, shouted from the driver's seat: "Hit them with the spoons!". My mother grabbed two heavy leaden spoons . . . and smashed down on the attackers' hands . . . My mother told me she stood shaking in the back of the van, holding the metal spoons dripping with blood and ice-cream . . . She developed a mistrust of Protestants which never left her, although she rarely expressed anger or overt bitterness towards them, and always told me that there were good Protestants as well as "bad ones". [Collins, 1997, pp. 31–32]

A Kleinian interpretation of this incident can be made.

In the story the ice-cream van symbolically represents the Catholic breast, which was milking the Orangemen at their March. This was too much to take for the Protestant state of mind and the good breast became the bad breast. A huge emotional shift occurred where the giver became the persecutor. This activated the primitive aggressive impulses that were dormant in the Protestant state of mind and that underlie *all* troubled minds in Northern Ireland. The bully took over and sanity was lost. Alcohol was the poison that released the emotional toxins.

For real change to occur, people have to take responsibility in day-to-day relationships for a containing rather than an aggressive response to hostile and suspicious emotions.

Victim transference

Finding an identity out of suffering has been identified as one of the main dysfunctional reactions to trauma. Van der Kolk and Van der Hart write:

Some traumatised people remain preoccupied with the trauma at the expense of other life experiences and continue to recreate it in some form for themselves or for others. Clinically these people are observed to have a vague sense of apprehension, emptiness, boredom and anxiety when not involved in activities reminiscent of the trauma. [Van der Kolk & Van der Hart, 1989, p. 399]

In Northern Ireland we talk of the victims' industry and the hierarchy of victims. Either people are making money out of forming victims' groups or some people's suffering is seen as higher than others. Human suffering becomes a contest or a money-making machine. How much more can the life instinct be hijacked by destructiveness to pervert compassion by seeking attention and pursuing self-aggrandisement? Facing a victim with the possibility of their suffering being used as a ploy to get attention demands considerable courage, as described in my paper on Omagh (Kapur, 2001). For the psychotic personality to face reality, such enormous hatred is stirred up that there is a wish to destroy the person representing this painful truth. For the victim to move into the depressive position requires relinquishing the attention gained from the trauma and giving up a special place in the eyes of others, most often the media. Addiction to the limelight deals temporarily with the emotional emptiness of their lives. A typical victim caught in this role sees others as:

- not knowing what it feels like to be traumatized;
- uncaring, for not dedicating every moment and ounce of energy to understanding their position;
- potential vultures feeding off the pain of their suffering so they can gain attention.

The victim transference also delivers considerable omnipotence. Others can be controlled and bullied by highlighting the pain and suffering of their position. Unfortunately, reinforcement of the transference through responding to this emotional intimidation never leads to resolution of the original loss. This mourning process is the only gateway to the depressive position.

A patient describes how being the victim of British oppression provided an opportunity for identity and excitement.

It was the early hours of the morning and the streets were pitch black. The street lighting had long been turned off to try to avoid or at least hamper IRA sniper attacks on British soldiers. The night silence was broken by the shrill of whistle blowing and bin-lid banging. The early warning system had kicked in, alerting the district that the "Brits" were raiding. I was up, dressed and out the door before my parents could stir from their bed. I stopped at the bin-shed to "arm" myself with my bin-lid and then I was off into the darkness. The eruption of noise and sheer exhilaration propelled me through the streets. I was 14 years old—no-one could stop me.

Self-esteem and inner strength is gained from standing up to the oppressor. The victim role gives life. Also, as stated earlier, these experiences of victimization provide the seeds for moral justification for acts of revenge. Victims, via the mechanism of projective identification described in Chapter Two make others experience and feel what they themselves experience and feel. This can lead to a wish for merger with others who themselves become unwitting victims of the trauma experience being replicated in others. Often, this is linked to the degree of helplessness surrounding the original event. For example, in natural disasters such as earthquakes and hurricanes, there is no one person or political system to blame. In contrast, in terrorist incidents the state did not protect its citizens and/or a group or another country was responsible for the trauma. This often vindicates the paranoid–schizoid functioning of the victim, where splitting is massive so that all the bad can be projected into the enemy. The unthinkable thought (Bion, 1962) is that they may bear some responsibility for their actions, and also they may be denying their own ambivalent feelings about the person who was killed. Cohen (2001) addresses the complexity of these victim dynamics when he writes:

"They started it" is the primeval account for private violence. The offender's claim to be the "real victim" refers to immediate, short-term defence and provocation. In political atrocities, denial of the victim is more ideologically rooted in historically interminable narratives of blaming the other. Recent spirals of virulent political violence all draw on the refrain of "Look what they did/are doing to us". [Cohen, 2001, p. 96]

An in-depth analysis of this style of relating reveals not only the complex manic defence structure of control, contempt, and triumph, but also a deep-down feeling of loss that cannot be mourned. This mourning may be about the loss of a loved one or the loss of a relationship that might have been, whether that is husband–wife, father–son or mother–daughter. The investment in "getting the other" can be a defence against unbearable feelings of not having a relationship with the loved one that the bereaved person would have liked.

As stated throughout this book, justification can be found for any event; a victim's experience is no different. A report from a social worker assigned to a victim of trauma in Northern Ireland highlights the intensity of these projective processes.

> I want you to feel what I feel. You will never know what it's like for me. Don't even try to understand. I will get my revenge in my own way.

Distrust: "Whatever you say, say nothing"

> Even in the relatively healthy individual, however, oral or anal anxieties may be clearly presented in the transference situation in the first session. Thus, a candidate [student] started the session by declaring his determination to be qualified in the minimum time and to get in all the analysis he could in the shortest possible time. Later in the session he spoke of his digestive troubles and, in another context, of cows, presenting a picture of his phantasy about the relation to the analyst so clearly as to enable me to make the interpretation that I was the cow, like the mother who breast-fed him, and that he felt he was going to empty me greedily, as fast as possible, of all my analysis—milk; this interpretation immediately brought out material about his guilt in relation to exhausting and exploiting his mother. [Segal, 1981/1985, p. 10]

While within a training context, this report from the eminent psycho-analyst, Hanna Segal, highlights day-to-day paranoid anxieties carried around by all of us. Within the controlled setting of a psychoanalytic session, the style of human relations unfolds where someone trained in interpretation can put words to the state of mind emerging in the consulting room. We all carry around these anxieties. However, when a human mind is exposed to intense experiences of violence these feelings of distrust become heightened. In the above "normal" example the patient wants a superficial relationship with the analyst (part-object) to extract knowledge without getting too close and then he is on his way. This manic defence hides a deep fear of intimacy that can be traced back to the primary relationship with his mother. In Northern Ireland we can trace this back to parental and societal experiences that were and are hostile and aggressive.

Northern Ireland is filled with stories of distrust. Communities have been polarized by so many experiences of violence and hatred that paranoia and suspicion is bound to form the leading edge of human relationships. Here, you deduce the religion of the other by making an immediate judgement on first meeting them based on their names. For example, common Catholic first names are Patrick, Eugene, Aoine, Majella, Brendan; Irish names, or those of a saint. Common Protestant names are William/Billy, Cedric, Ivan, or display a tendency to use a surname as a first name, such as Carson, Wilson, Johnston, Montgomery. Names associated with the Royal family, well known political or British army figures from the past are all recognized as "Protestant". As there are always exceptions to this rule, categorization can also occur by how a person may pronounce the letter "h", Protestants pronouncing the letter as "aitch".

All these and many more day-today nuances highlight the deep levels of distrust that lead people to "say nothing". Kapur (2002), in an unpublished study, found that people could not attend group therapy sessions for trauma because they were too frightened to say what they felt and thought in case people found out they were from the "other side" and they would then face persecution. Fears of retaliation are intense. In Northern Ireland society, organizations, groups, and individuals provide few opportunities for members to experience trust, particularly in the face of alternative or contrasting belief systems. Objects which differ from the projector become convenient recipients for doubt and suspicion. This leads to what is known in Northern Ireland as the "siege mentality", where each group hides away from the other for fear of attack. In this state of mind powerful negative images and phantasies build up about the other side. A well-known joke illustrates this process.

A Protestant homeowner wants to cut his lawn. His mower is broken and as he lives in the countryside his nearest neighbour is the only person nearby who has a mower. He is a Catholic. He ponders for days and days as to whether he should approach this Catholic neighbour for use of his mower. Meanwhile, the grass gets longer. The Protestant makes several attempts to summon up the courage to call. This goes on for weeks until he can bear the height of his overgrown lawn no longer. He marches up furiously to the Catholic owned house, knocks furiously on the door and says to the bemused Catholic homeowner "I didn't want your bloody lawn-mower anyway". All before his Catholic neighbour has a chance to open his mouth.

This comical story hides more sinister unconscious phantasies that make up everyday life here. Catholics and Protestants come to very rapid conclusions about the intentions, feelings, and motivations of the other side. As Segal highlights, these are present in everyday life in a "normal" society, but in a society like Northern Ireland there is "double trouble" for the man or woman in the street. Mitrani (2001, p. 41) highlights this again in her excellent text *Ordinary People and Extra-Ordinary Projections* by quoting the work of the well-known analyst Frances Tustin: "As therapists our task is to help our patients towards humaness when so much of the time the ordinariness of being human is not available to them".

Mitrani herself comments that:

Quite frequently, in those ordinary adults seen in today's practice of analysis, a degree of circumventing an area of amputated development that has been callused over or encapsulated. As one patient put it: "I have this hole—an empty spot deep inside me—maybe I'm just afraid to find that nothing is there". This patient, whom I call Hendrick—an overtly angry and bullying man—seemed to cover over these holes with a chip on his shoulder. Eventually we came to understand this "chip" or callused cynical attitude and tough bullying behaviour, as a "chip off the old block"; which referred to his feelings about his father. One day, this patient lamented "He protected me, but he just didn't seem to know what to do with me when I couldn't throw the ball right. He thought I was a sissy—I threw the ball like a girl". [Mitrani, 2001, p. 43]

Could it be that because of the fear of intimacy, lots of people in Northern Ireland carry around deep black holes that become expressed as aggressive, bullying behaviour? Have we bred individuals who use the classic manic defences of control, triumph, and contempt to hide deep down inadequacies born out of having few, if any, intimate human relations where they could be filled up with real emotional growth? My thesis is that this is very much the case. Paranoid–schizoid functioning has covered over the cracks of a superficial style of relating because of the deep-down fear of being annihilated by the other side. Unless and until we can be more vulnerable with each other and invest in softness and humanity, we will continue archaic and suspicious styles of relating. It is particularly important that those in authority take responsibility to be role models as "gentle men" rather than "hard men". Only then will individuals have an opportunity fill deep inner black holes with real human warmth.

Poisonous projections

Anyone tuning in to the radio and television or reading the papers can easily see the blame culture that dominates everyday relationships in Northern Ireland. We are a society that believes if we force others to own up to their crimes everything will be resolved. These projections are so poisonous that powerful negative feelings are constantly located in others. There emerges a hot pursuit of the truth located in the other person. The legal and political system here institutionalizes this blame game. Rules and regulations are constructed around finding fault with others. Many examples in the peace process highlight this toxic style of relationship.

• If the IRA disarm/disband everything will be OK (how about the dominant Unionist community owning up to institutionalized oppression and injustice?).
• If the Unionists stop saying NO, everything will be OK (how about the Nationalists owning up to their impulse to triumph over their enemy?).

This political discourse will then find its way into daily life. Unconsciously, having witnessed this negative coupling on television, people will re-enact this scene in their personal and work relationships. The case of the police Ombudsman versus the Chief

Constable highlights this violent parental blame game. Either the Ombudsman had to own up to RUC bashing or the Chief Constable had to own up to professional negligence. How about each player asking the question, "what is it in me that contributed to the conflict?" This "retrieving of projections" is rare in day-to-day life in a troubled society. Unfortunately, it is the only way out of the cycle of emotional violence that gives people the justification to detoxify the other side by attacking their homes or murdering their loved ones. Public figures and everyone in day-to-day life have to begin to retrieve the poisonous emotions they put into others in order to see real evidence of the psychological peace process so necessary for the political process to succeed.

A cartoon in the *Evening Standard* (Figure 4) accurately summarizes the madness of this process. Sadism, the pleasure gained in inflicting pain, is rife in everyday relationships. Whether it is with bullets or words, killing off the life in others through putting your worst into others is accepted as normal. An excerpt from the UVF Military Policy clearly locates the enemy "out there":

Figure 4.   JAK cartoon, London *Evening Standard,* 29 October 1982

In order to destroy the forces of terrorism and subversion the Ulster Volunteer Force is pledged to:

(a) Track down and eliminate the Command Structure of the enemy.
(b) Seek out and destroy enemy active service personnel.
(c) Uncover and disrupt enemy supplies and sources of finance.
(d) Harrass and intimidate those who give shelter and support to the enemy. [Sinnerton, 2002]

An unthinkable thought aimed at retrieving projections would be to accept our own propensity to terrorize *and* realize that when we abuse authority we create the breeding ground for terrorist states of mind.

A "Loyalist" poem taken from Stone's book highlights the complete location of blame on to the other:

Loyalist

When I was just a boy
This bloody war was begun
With a rebellious violence
Which killed and stunned
Indiscriminate terrorists
Still slash and scar
With sectarian attacks
On Protestant bars
Bombs of destruction
Tear the heart out of my city
Bloody Friday, Enniskillen
They never showed any pity
Republican death squads
Spawned from hell
In ethnic-cleansing, they do excel
These hooded cowards
With hate-filled eyes
Create the horror
Ignore the cries
Now a man
I've answered the call
I am an Ulster Freedom Fighter, defender and all.

[Stone, 2003, p. 26]

Is there any space to retrieve these projections? In a recent book, the journalist Brian Rowan features a conversation between himself and Stone.

> *Stone*—I would share in that [apologizing] most definitely. I have said in the past that all deaths are regrettable, be they innocent civilians, members of the Security Forces, Loyalist volunteers and yes, even members of the Republican death squads.
>
> *Rowan*—Do you apologise for what you did?
>
> *Stone*—Within the context of being a volunteer in a war, no, I don't apologise, but I acknowledge the hurt I've caused. [Rowan, 2003, p. 139]

This is an important step towards the depressive position and a movement towards the retrieval of locating evil in the other. In many ways, Northern Ireland is "ahead of the game" in being able to see the human destructiveness we have inflicted on each other and now recognizing the wastefulness of this. These important moves cannot be underestimated as they are the only way to achieve a psychological process where human relations can be normalized to a peaceful state of mind characterized by concern rather than hate.

Complex containment

Northern Ireland is contained not only by its own civic leaders but also the politics of London, Dublin, and Washington. How these parental figures contain and detoxify the state of mind of Northern Ireland has a huge impact on the political future. Effective containment requires patience and thinking through complex emotional issues. Often the three parental players have failed in this task.

- London has forgotten its history of colonialism and imposed decisions which are felt to be good for Northern Ireland people.
- Dublin has treated Northern Ireland as a deviant child that needs to "wise up".
- Washington has changed its views on terrorism after September 11 and expects Unionists to trust them after years of their supporting the IRA as "freedom fighters".

Northern Ireland is at the mercy of clumsy containment by players who have not yet worked out their own inadequacies and contradictions. Stable containment, like stable parenting, requires a thoughtful and rational approach that is not influenced by national agendas. Often Northern Ireland has had to contain the inadequacies and deviance of these other players, who are sent to sort out this "recalcitrant child". All interfaces in the political processes have to be devoid of personal/national agendas. Otherwise Northern Ireland will only become the left-over container of other nations' problems. This focuses serious attention on the detail of how political players relate to Northern Ireland. Using the province as a pawn in another game will only add poison to an already full container of unprocessed primitive emotions.

All of our parental figures have coupled badly. The peace process is threatened by a "blow-job" in the White House. This undermines the psychic, healthy, mature, adult coupling required for creative human relations. In the minds of many people in Northern Ireland the peace process seems based more on the needy and greedy appetites of politicians than it is on the real casualties of human destructiveness. Politicians in America, the UK, and Ireland are neglecting their human responsibilities when they provide such poor role models of human sexuality. This is not being moralistic. People traumatized by violence can place little faith in politicians preoccupied with their own desires rather than with real concern for the people damaged by violence. Perverse coupling is the territory of the paranoid–schizoid failing to accept responsibility for their shortcomings. The implications of role models in our society not accepting responsibility for their failings leaves a society lacking in basic trust. Everyone, particularly civic leaders, has to take seriously the responsibility to live as much as possible in the depressive position.

To reiterate the points raised in Chapter One, we quote Sean Farren, a member of the Social Democratic and Labour Party and previously Minister for Finance in the Northern Ireland Assembly, who underlines the dysfunctional relationships that require this complex containment.

Northern Ireland was, therefore, from its inception, deeply divided in virtually every aspect of communal life, its deep patterns of

segregation most readily identifiable in terms of religious affiliation. . . . Relationships between Unionist administrations and the
British Government throughout this period tended to be distant,
exactly as the Unionist Party preferred, and the British themselves
were happy to allow . . . London, maintained, therefore, the traditional distance which is generally evident in metropole-settler relationships during periods of political calm, respecting its side of the
covenant into which it had entered with Unionists in 1921. . . .
North–South relationships had become even more distant as both
parts of Ireland grew steadily apart in the years following the country's partition. [Farren & Mulvihill, 2000, pp. 17–18]

So where were the good enough parents (Winnicott, 1979)?
London was turning a blind eye to the political and democratic
murder of the rights of Catholics as the bad Unionist parent was left
to get on with its implicit and explicit oppression. And what about
the distant Uncle Sam? Farren comments on the imposition of
internment that Dublin appealed to this "blood relative" for help.

The British Government resented Dublin's criticism of what its
subordinate regional Government in Northern Ireland was doing,
especially when that criticism was vehemently expressed abroad,
particularly to powerful and sympathetic politicians in the United
States. [Farren & Mulvihill, 2000, p. 55]

Emotionally, pressure on the USA did lead to the Good Friday
Agreement, where we can see some semblance of better parenting
and acknowledging the complex containment that needed to take
place to achieve a state of mind where mutual dependence is seen as
the way forward. Here, the rights and views of Nationalists and
Unionists have been seriously recognized by Northern Ireland's
British and Irish parents and a helpful Uncle Sam in the guise of
President Clinton and Senator Mitchell's efforts. There is still much
work to do but the Good Friday Agreement did, for the first time,
begin to equalize the relationships between the two warring factions.

Criminal versus natural justice

The outcome of failed containment is the implementation of unjust
and unfair laws. There emerges a legitimization of oppression and

dominance that persuades even the most ordinary and law-abiding people to take up arms. As documented earlier by Eamon Collins, there are plenty of experiences of real injustice to sow the seeds of terrorism. A patient describes her experience of confronting British oppression.

> Crowds of young men were stoning the soldiers. The "Brits" were firing rubber bullets into the crowd at short range, aiming for their heads rather than the lower body as they were supposed to do. The air was thick with smoke from hi-jacked cars and vans parked at angles on the road. I watched from a distance, waiting on the signal. Then it came. I quickly hurried along the street towards the house, up the stairs into the bedroom. I stood on a chair and opened the roofspace door, feeling for the familiar round tins. I removed two nail-bombs from their hiding place and pushed them into the waistband of my skirt at the small of my back. My coat hung loosely around me to hide the tell-tale bulge. I hurried back to where I had been, to watch the signal being given for the crowd to quickly disperse before the "tins of beans" were thrown.

The accepted way of achieving justice is either through the legal system or, as above, by people taking up arms. In both situations there is an onus for a "pound of flesh" whether this is obtained through the Courts or by taking up violence. I suggest a new way. Natural justice. Relying on life to naturally correct and repay human criminality takes pressure off the victim to find justice and allows everyday life to "right the wrong". Massive investment in retribution takes its toll on the individual or group wanting "blood", or their view of the truth to be upheld. The "Bloody Sunday" Enquiry highlights this. While undoubtedly an injustice has been done to those murdered, people are looking to a legal process for "closure". This will only happen through the difficult work of the depressive position, where there is mourning for loved ones and a giving up of revenge. Otherwise lives are lost through an indefinite preoccupation with seeking justice, with the false premise of substituting a legal process for a complex emotional process of giving up people and ideas. A belief in natural justice reinvests hope in the life instinct rather than in eternal preoccupation with "getting even".

So many injustices have taken place in Northern Ireland. The normal course of action has been through the legal system, which has created a culture of many people devoting their life to "getting their pound of flesh" in the courts. This is a huge investment of time and energy. The alternative route to natural justice allows, in Klenian terminology, a switch from the death instinct to the life instinct. Potentially, this can be seen by the victim as denying the extent of their suffering. A public acknowledgement is seen as the only way to resolve the injustice. Cohen highlights this usual method of seeking justice, commenting on its limitations:

> From the Nuremberg trials fifty years ago to the current International Criminal Tribunals (for Rwanda and the former Yugoslavia) to the future International Criminal court, the standard issues of justice and retribution are the same. Two sub-issues are relevant here.
>
> Firstly, must collective truth-telling always lead to justice because individual moral responsibility is essential to the truth? Mainstream human rights policy is clear: we investigate the past in order to identify those responsible and bring them to legal account. We know that this seldom happens. There has been no historical episode where anything remotely like a full policy of criminal accountability has been implemented. Amnesties are granted (secretly or openly) as a condition of regime change. Truth telling is not the beginning of coming to terms with the past, but all there is. There is no political will to go further; the enquiry drags on endlessly; evidence is destroyed; witnesses somehow lose their memory; investigators turn out to be corrupt, intimidated or connected to the security forces; the criminal justice system is hopelessly weak and inefficient. And hovering above is the residual power of the old regime, the risk that prosecutions would jeopardize fragile democratic gains.
>
> There is a second, less familiar, issue; not whether recovering the past "must" lend to legal accountability, but whether criminal law is at all helpful in recovery. To convert private knowledge to public acknowledgement, are the rituals of accusation, proof, attribution of blame and punishment necessary? [Cohen, 2001, pp. 228–229]

The alternative route of natural justice disinvests energy from this technical pursuit of criminal justice and potentially frees the individual to begin the painful process of mourning. It may be that in Northern Ireland we need both, but one (criminal justice) without the other (natural justice) seems to ignore the lessons of history. The external world recognizing the suffering of the internal will not lead to "closure". In many ways, it may postpone forever the painful mourning process that victims have to go through to reach the depressive position.

Envy and inadequacy

Envy is a silent killer. It is most prevalent in relationships where people cannot bear the success of others. However, when we are left feeling inadequate we invariably feel this is because we are indeed failing in some part of ourselves. Certain conditions usually exist when a person is left feeling useless and inferior.

● The person who believes they are superior has to have an inferior/inadequate part of themselves that they cannot bear which has to be relocated in the other.
● The recipient of the projection of inadequacy often is carrying around an intense feeling of inferiority that catches the projection.

Of course, we all carry around inadequate parts of ourselves. It is when we can no longer bear these feelings that they get sent to someone else. This is often triggered through envy of the other person. In the counter-transference we are left experiencing the negative feelings of the other person.

As stated earlier, Northern Ireland is a split society. This is seen no more so than in the academic and professional snobbery of the middle classes. To be a doctor or similar professional is to be better than the ordinary man. This idealization presents non-professionals as ready-made toilets to be projected into. Hierarchical relationships are part and parcel of everyday life. What may spark off the projection of inadequacy by the professional is envy of creative talents that the non-professional may have. In my experience, the non-professionals are often more handsome and attractive than middle class snobs! In essence, creativity and emotional life are attacked by professionals, who often have schizoid relationships with others. They are cut off from real emotional life and manage this inadequacy by projecting into bricklayers, hairdressers, and plumbers.

An excerpt from Stone's book on his experience of school summarizes this split, which sows the seeds of inadequacy, and ultimately terrorism, against a dominant and oppressive object.

> My school years—I went to primary school which was right oppo-
> site my home—were not the happiest of my life. I preferred school-
> yard games to sitting behind a desk and doing my lessons . . . one
> teacher ensured I would leave school with little education and a
> dislike bordering on a hatred for teachers and educators. Bordering
> on Braniel estate was a middle-class estate called Glenview and
> children from there also attended Braniel Primary. The teacher was
> a snob: he held a senior position of responsibility but believed
> working-class kids had no right to education. He ran the school
> with an iron fist.

> I had one encounter with this teacher which shaped the rest of my
> school life. When I was eight he slapped me in the face, causing my
> nose to bleed profusely. He beat me because I took a fit of giggles
> in the playground when we were lining up to go back into class. I
> have never forgotten or forgiven the incident. [Stone, 2003, p. 11]

The cure for these silent attacks is for all of us to own up to our imperfections, value talents in others that we don't have in ourselves, and be content with our lot. As envy is such a deep killer of other people's confidence it takes a huge effort to stop hating in others what we can't have in ourselves. It is only when we quietly take pride in our own achievements and admire the talents of others that we can truly experience the depressive position.

Envy and inadequacy also get "acted out" in relationships of infantile rather than mutual dependency. Could it be that the Ulster baby remains in an infantile dependent relationship with its British mother? This is a ready-made vehicle for the British projecting their negative states of mind into Northern Ireland and for Northern Ireland not finding its independence, as it feels unable to do so. I believe this pattern of personal relationships is repeated in day-to-day life.

- Husbands and wives set up such dependencies, where one partner becomes the dominant father or mother figure.

- "Hard-man" management styles perpetuate this type of relationship; in my experience I have felt like little black Sambo surrounded by the big white chiefs.
- Professional relationships, as stated earlier, have an inherent infantilization, with the high-brow professional entering into a paternal relationship with the patient or lay person.

A clinical example illustrates the existence of envy in therapeutic work. A male patient in his thirties would often speak of the hard edge to his personality, which he described like a "flint" ready to cut the therapist to pieces. He could shoot or bomb the therapist at any time and, like paramilitaries, his was the element of surprise. This hardness was like a protective security screen, which would ward off potential murderous attacks by others, particularly the therapist. It felt as though he was gathering "intelligence" to find out the therapist's Achilles' heel and plan an attack accordingly. The therapist always parked his car, which was fitted with child seats, in a nearby car park. Would the patient's envy push him into viewing this as something that he could attack? This "hard man" personality structure can engulf sane and rational personality processes to such an extent that an internal intimidation takes place between the psychotic/envious and non-psychotic/creative parts of his personality, whereby any experience of growth or development can immediately be kidnapped and held hostage by the hard man. The following interchange illustrates this point.

> *Patient*: Well the thing is, sometimes I can be positive, optimistic, and then like today, I feel pessimistic, I feel nothing helps, no one can understand my difficulties. This pessimistic side is full of doom and gloom. If you can imagine that my pessimistic side consists of thousands of soldiers, never-ending, who tell me that everything is bad, no one can help. These endless thoughts tell me that I want help. Nothing can save me from the overwhelming pessimism, and then, the most optimistic side of my personality gets pushed out. These negative feelings and thoughts just keep marching into my mind.

> *Therapist*: I think you are letting me know of the tremendous internal struggle that goes on in your mind between the part of you that wants to come here and has found the sessions helpful and this more negative side which convinces you that I'm no good, I can't possibly understand, I'm useless.

Patient: Well, it's in all aspects of my life, in my job, in my relationship with my wife, this pessimistic side keeps on saying these good experiences are not for me, they're not going to make me feel any better, they begin to say that this therapist, this psychologist is no good. He may seem confident that he can help me, but maybe I'll be the one out of a hundred he can't help. Anyway, my pessimistic side says it can gather together an army to attack my optimism in my relationship to you.

Bion (1959a) points to the inevitability of envious attacks on constructive links—the example above illustrates how a powerful internal army can be immediately mobilized against the threat of positive change. In Northern Ireland we can see rare situations where agreement has been reached and then the proposed resolution of conflict breaks down. Our thesis is that, intra-psychically, the hard man may feel so pushed out and enraged by the presence of rational constructive dialogue that he attacks any possibility of agreement; to do otherwise would represent weakness and the ultimate demise of the identity of the hard man. Politically, it may then be wiser to have realistic ambitions about the amount of change that can actually take place when such internal forces are mobilized to prevent constructive change. It may be that, as with working with severe mental illness, only small changes to Northern Irish society are possible, with the acceptance of the inevitability of attacks on progress. Perhaps the caution around the current peace talks is a more realistic response to the prospect of an army of psychotic personalities having to surrender their psychological weapons immediately—as Gerry Adams said of the IRA, "They haven't gone away, you know!"

Conclusion

In global politics hopes for peace and resolution of conflicts are invariably projected into politicians. However, as any peacemaker knows, there has to be a bottom-up approach that meets the top-down approach half way. This is where the onus is on us as individuals to relate differently to each other. More harmonious human relations can be achieved by creating states of mind where people in everyday life—

- take responsibility for leaving people with our projected bad feelings;
- do not force their views on to others through fear, intimidation, and threat, which is another form of terrorism for the middle-classes;
- do not play victim when things go wrong in order to control the minds of others;
- take responsibility when things go wrong rather than looking for others to change;
- do not make an already toxic state of mind more poisonous by playing out their personal agendas;
- accept that we all have a troubled mind that makes life miserable for others.

We can no longer disown our capacity and responsibility to repair a troubled mind. This individual awareness is the only way out of a troubled mind in ourselves. The Eastern philosopher, Jiddu Krishnamurti, writes of this moment-to-moment meditation as the only way to give up human destructiveness as follows:

When you learn about yourself, watch the way you walk, how you eat, what you say, the gossip, the hate, the jealousy—if you are aware of all that in yourself, without any choice, that is part of meditation. [Krishnamurti, 1983, p. 59]

CHAPTER FIVE

Working with groups affected by the Troubles

G roup processes are powerful vehicles for people to commit destructive acts without a recognition of the human effects of their action. Freud brought our attention to these processes when he wrote of the herd or gang instinct, whereby a group becomes so possessed with an idea that any destructive act is possible. Bion (1959b) took these ideas forward and describes three destructive processes that are characteristic of negative groups. He suggested that some groups can be in a work group mode similar to depressive position functioning, where people are engaging in a rational and thoughtful way to find a constructive and non-psychotic resolution to their problems. In contrast, a negative group is characterized by three states of mind. First, there is a state where group members depend on the leader for all the answers (basic assumption dependency). Second, they pair up to provide a third personality to overthrow the group leader (basic assumption pairing). Here the Oedipal impulse, which refers to the Greek myth of the son wishing to overthrow his father to join with his mother, is acted out. Britton *et al.* (1989) have written on the clinical implications of this. The relevance of the concept here is to highlight the emotional surge from a group to get rid of the leader and replace it with one of its own. This phantasy is acted out through two people pairing to form a couple, producing a new baby which replaces the leader. The third state of mind is referred to as the fight–flight. There is a wish for group members either to fight with each other or to flee.

In these descriptions Bion (1959b) uses the phrase "basic assumption" to refer to the primitive impulses that drive the group to act negatively. This negative process also occurs when a group becomes too cohesive and acts as a cult with extreme religious fervour (Yalom, 1985). In this state of mind, there is little or no room for disagreement. The leader has to be obeyed through the idealization of hierarchical authority. In contrast, too little cohesiveness leads to a fragmentation of the group and a diminished sense of belonging associated with a fight–flight impulse.

Recently, Kernberg (2003a,b) has added to this analysis of group processes by elucidating the more regressive aspects of groups that can reinforce dysfunctional leadership. In adding to the concepts of dependency and fight–flight groups he adds:

A narcissistic regression of the group (corresponding to Bion's "dependent group") stimulates the emergence of a narcissistic, self-congratulatory, self-assured leader, who thrives on the admiration of others and assumes the role of an "all-giving" parental authority, on whom everybody else can depend for sustenance and security. In the throes of its regression, the group's members become passive and dependent upon that leader, and assume that it is their right to be fed and taken care of . . .

A group involved in a paranoid regression conforms to Bion's descriptions of the "fight–flight basic assumption group". It becomes hyper-alert and tense, as if there were some danger against which it would have to establish an aggressive defence. The group selects a leader with a strong paranoid potential, a hyper-sensitive, suspicious, aggressive and dominant person, ready to experience and define some slight or danger against which he and the group following him need to protect themselves and fight back. The members of the group, in turn, tend to divide between an "in-group", rallying around the group leader, and an "out group" who are suspect and need to be fought off. The mutual recriminations and fights between the "in group" and the "out group" give a frankly hostile and paranoid quality to the entire group, and may

lead either to splitting into paranoid splinter groups, or the discov-
ery of an external enemy against whom the entire group can consol-
idate around the leader. The fight then evolves between that
paranoid group and the external world. [Kernberg, 2003a, p. 685]

We will explore this further in respect of how these styles of
leadership can be found in Northern Ireland and elsewhere.

Leadership

Narcissistic

We find this both in the troubled mind of Northern Ireland and in
many other regions of the world. We see in many totalitarian
regimes the need for idealization of the dictator, from Mussolini
to Saddam Hussein, and the fulfilment of their narcissistic needs
through constant adulation. In Northern Ireland this style of leadership is evident, particularly within more extreme Unionism. The
speeches of the Reverend Ian Paisley are legendary, in which he
calls upon his flock not only to follow him blindly, but to bestow
unquestioning, positive adulations. This fix into a chronic dependency on the leader leads to a cult-like following that never questions his actions. This may also be reinforced by the infantile
dependent relationship with the British state. The reliance on direct
rule has lead to a culture of "they know best across the water". This
becomes evident in all forms of public life, from universities to the
health services. Of course, Britain, struggling with the loss of its
imperial past, soaks up such sources of narcissism as a way of
coping with its lost colonial authority. Citizens of Northern Ireland
have a responsibility to minimize the projection of authority inside
and outside its own boundaries to stop the leakage of authority and
confidence to its own state of mind. Importantly, local leaderships
and British leadership have to give back authority and not steal or
poach talents and abilities that are not their own.

Paranoid

Again, we see many examples of this, particularly in the construction of paramilitary groups where the enemy is always on the

outside. This, of course, becomes so embedded in day-to-day human relations that dehumanization sets in, thus justifying killing others. Whether it is Tianamen Square in China, or the assassination of political opponents and "military targets" in Northern Ireland, a paranoid leader suspiciously gathers enough evidence to justify his or her acts of destruction. In Northern Ireland we have seen the splits that Kernberg refers to in both Republican and Loyalist groups when they have killed their own. Surely this highlights the powerfulness of unconscious primitive aggressive forces over political leadership or ideology. When Protestants are killing Protestants and Catholics are killing Catholics, the projection and splitting of suspicion and aggression has become most clear.

Here, we now see the Provisional IRA having their own conflicts with the Continuity or Real IRA. We also see the UVF competing with the UDA and the Red Hand Commandos, leading to in-fighting feuds and murder. When paranoid leadership is flourishing, death and destruction takes over all group processes. Politically, we see this within the recent history of the Ulster Unionist Party, whose leader faces constant threats of a coup from younger, stronger, more high profile members of his party, all eager to replace the master. Each attack is met with a re-grouping and a sad, desperate fight for survival that also sends out a message to his followers—is it now time to move allegiance?

In proposing a model of leadership across all groups, whether they are organizations or political leaderships, Kernberg proposes five characteristics:

Functional leadership combines the following characteristics, (1) high intelligence, enabling the leader to apply long range strategic thinking to diagnosing, formulating, communicating and implementing the requirements of the task within its constraints; (2) sufficient emotional maturity and human depth to be able to assess the personality of others in selecting subordinate leaders and delegating appropriate authority to them; (3) a solid and deep moral integrity that protects the leader from the unavoidable temptations intimately linked to the exercise of power and from the corrupting pressures of the leader's entourage; (4) sufficiently strong narcissistic tendencies to be able to maintain self-esteem in the face of unavoidable criticism and attacks of the followers, and to avoid depending upon the followers for fulfillment of excessive narcissistic needs; (5) sufficient paranoid features—in contrast to naivete—to diagnose early the unavoidable ambivalent and hostile undercurrents in the organisation that express the resentful, rebellious and envious aspects of the aggression directed toward the leadership. [Kernberg, 2003a, pp. 692–693]

A tall order! Kernberg goes on to highlight his own paradox: don't be paranoid and narcissistic but be paranoid and narcissistic enough to survive the inevitable basic assumption/primitive negative functioning that is part of any group process. This task is difficult enough within a "normal" society, but add this into a troubled society like Northern Ireland and you have few, if any, role models of wise leaders who can conduct themselves in a thoughtful, careful, creative, but essentially non-paranoid, and non-narcissistic role. Unfortunately though, this is the only style of leadership that can move us to depressive position functioning. The onus is on all leaders, political and civic, to take responsibility for their style of relating to promote more positive work group functioning, where intimate and affectionate human relationships can prosper.

I will now illustrate how these more negative processes are most prevalent in the troubled mind of Northern Ireland. A work group state of mind with healthy cohesiveness is a rare occurrence when a society has been exposed to such destructiveness. In my view it would constitute only 10–20% of all group processes in everyday human relations in Northern Ireland.

Destructiveness and religion

Religion can be good and bad. Used well it acts as a benevolent state that guides people through the ups and downs of life and fosters an atmosphere where they are good to their neighbour. Christianity is expressed through good acts to our fellow man. This is rare in the troubled mind of Northern Ireland. Here religion has been hijacked to think badly about, and behave badly to, others. This split is common in all similar conflicts. Whether it be Catholics or Protestants, Muslims or Hindus, or Jews and Arabs, religion can be hijacked by society to justify harm to others. This is where religion becomes a mental illness, a form of schizophrenia in which there is a danger of others being harmed.

When religion is hijacked by the psychotic personality anything is possible. Usually, a leader emerges who demands the unquestioning obedience of his or her flock. We see this in both Protestant and Catholic religions. For Protestants in Northern Ireland, the most famous political leader is Dr Ian Paisley. For Catholics, idealization ranges from the priests to politicians like Gerry Adams. In these destructive processes there is no room for questioning and debate. Disagreement leads to the person going to hell (accordingly, I have my place booked!) The most severe persecutions are visited on those that lose their faith.

To highlight the abuse of authority when society enters into a basic assumption dependency relationship with religious or other authority figures, I have taken an excerpt from an official Protestant paper, *The Banner of Ulster*, published in 1852.

So long as the aristocracy of this country shall be permitted to carry out the despotism which they have been in the habit of exercising over the electoral people, there neither is nor can be any effectual help for the counter evil necessarily generated by it, the highly unnatural and dangerous growth of an ecclesiastical–secular power of Roman Catholic priests, it is the unconstitutional dominion of landlordism which puts power into the Priests' hands and it is worse than futile to lament over the consequent mischief, so long as men choose to protect the abuse in which that mischief had its primary origin. [Wright, 1996, p. 202]

Ireland, and Northern Ireland in particular, has a long history of people abusing their authority. Society falls into an idealized dependency with priests, landlords, and many other statues built on feet of clay. Priests, in particular, have been publicly exposed as abusing this authority through numerous scandals related to paedophilia.

The evangelical and right-wing Catholic styles of relatedness represent a cult dynamic with basic assumption dependent functioning. The words of the leader take on Godlike qualities and are followed strictly. To offer an alternative view would invite the wrath of an internal psychotic personality that intimidates the patient with death and destruction. A patient with a strong evangelical past said to me:

I'm going against God talking to you. If we continue these sessions you will die tomorrow. There is no doubt about that. You and I must stop speaking about my feelings. The devil in my mind cannot be questioned. You will go to hell.

The fear and intimidation communicated to me via projective identification was intense. I thought my life was in danger and I was going to die. Such is the fear and terror of the psychotic personality. It is only when these group processes can be questioned that we can move to a depressive position function where intimidation and fear is replaced by concern for others.

This structure of group functioning filters its way into all types of organization: hospitals, schools, businesses, and even terrorist groups.

As in any military structure there is complete trust in the leadership. This blind following leads to horrific acts of war and terrorism. Freud warned us to "never under-estimate the power of the need to obey". Classic research by the psychologist Milgram (1963) confirms this phenomenon. In a controlled laboratory environment more than sixty-five per cent of his subjects could be readily manipulated into inflicting a (seemingly) lethal electric charge on a total stranger. The subjects sincerely believed that they were causing great physical pain, but despite their victims' pitiful pleas for them to stop, sixty-five per cent continued to obey orders and increase the voltage until there could be little doubt their victims were dead. Even when the trappings of authority are no more than a white coat, Milgram elicited compliant responses from "normal" people to the instruction to inflict pain .

To dissolve this fantastic power of authority requires a different form of leadership. "Follow the Leader" has to be questioned, while also respecting the leader. Sinnerton describes the role of this transformational leadership when speaking of Gusty Spence.

> Spence continued to challenge the loyalists' preconceived notions of themselves. One has to be reminded the Loyalists were loth to be critical. Inherent in that very term "loyalist" lay a contradiction which inhibited open discussion: to whom or to what did they owe allegiance?

Eddie Kinner (another loyalist) explains their dilemma.

At that stage, a lot of us, because of our circumstances, were fighting to remain British, and all of a sudden we were now being punished by the British. We were being forced to question our own loyalty. There was a fear to do that openly, and it was Gusty [Spence] who brought that out in Long Kesh. He encouraged you to ask those questions. You weren't treacherous when you questioned the British Government and your own people and that then allowed the debates to take place within the cubicles. [Sinnerton, 2002, p. 49]

In object relations terms, fierce loyalty to the strict internal object that demands obedience means that any act can be justified or morality is lost. Good and evil become mixed up as there is a rationalization that doing harm to others will bring good. The primitive adhesion to aggressive internal objects is no different to that found in mental illness (Gabbard, 2000). So it is no surprise when Eamon Collins writes:

By the end of 1984, I had started to feel real fear. I fought hard to control it, but my nerves had started to fray. I was beginning to feel mentally ill, afflicted by a growing sense of awfulness of what I had done. [Collins, 1997, p. 244]

Kernberg underlines the power of these regressive forces in religion in his comments on how fundamental religious ideology can be used to justify dehumanization.

Fundamental ideologies divide the world into ideal and evil realms; their own ideology belongs to the ideal realm and its proponents are thus guaranteed goodness, survival and redemption; happiness, harmony and moral triumph. The ideas, beliefs and behaviour of the realm of evil are immoral, dangerous, destructive and threatening to everything that the good stand for. The triumph of the good and the destruction of evil will bring about universal peace and harmony and the end to all conflicts and grievances. Typically, such an ideology projects all aggression on to the evil social group, while justifying aggression against the infidel as a necessary defence and retribution if not a moral imperative". [Kernberg, 2003b, p.56]

The relevance to Northern Ireland is clear. When one group takes a morally superior position, projection of evil on to the other allows for the most evil of acts.

Idealization of the death instinct

Finding an identity out of violence has become a way of life for many in Northern Ireland. The energy and excitement gained from destructive processes makes its way into day-to-day life, including sport. Some of our famous sporting heroes show all the signs of a death instinct that is alive and unwell. From George Best to Alex Higgins, we have produced sportsmen who love the limelight, booze, and women. While these sporting figures may have left Northern Ireland to pursue their careers in adulthood, their formative years took place in this unconscious atmosphere of idealization of aggression. Clubs and societies unwittingly reinforce violent human relationships as an ideal state of mind. It is no coincidence that Northern Ireland has one of the highest rates of professional soccer fouls/offences in the whole of the UK. "Kicking the shit out of someone" is the norm.

The manic defences of triumph, control, and contempt surround these sporting icons and their natural talents get hijacked by the psychotic personality that demands more buzz. We idealize these icons. In Northern Ireland we are not allowed to question the destructive correlates of talent. In motorbike racing we lost one of our best racers, Joey Dunlop, in road racing. We are one of the last countries in the world that supports this type of bike racing, which is more dangerous than track racing. The daredevil personality in all of us is accentuated by a troubled mind, which heightens the addiction to destructive relationships.

These sporting icons, and sport in general, becomes so destructive that it has a part-object relationship with the world. While all such sports as road racing carry high levels of risk, a fatal error leaves a bereaved family behind. High profile sportsmen often leave loved ones who struggle to mourn the loss of their relative because they have to try to deal with feelings of resentment that they are the ones who have lost out. The public may have vicariously experienced the excitement of the sport, but where is the parent of the children left behind when they most need them?

Other institutions and organizations also idealize the death instinct. As stated in Chapter Four, inadequacy is readily projected into those not belonging to a particular club. The power and the glory is projected into the establishment that controls many public bodies and private industry in Northern Ireland. For many years this was the control of the Unionist population, as Sean Farren, MLA, writes:

> To protect their own state against perceived internal dangers, successive Unionist Governments permitted and actively connived at a range of discriminatory practices aimed at diminishing as much as possible, Catholic Nationalist political influence, while at the same time consciously developing a sense of Britishness about life in Northern Ireland. [Farren & Mulvihill, 2000, p. 19]

In the creation of the Northern Ireland state there are many examples of destructiveness being institutionalized in the shape of legitimized oppression. Farren and Mulvihill elaborate:

> Both in terms of Northern Ireland's creation and in the manner in which it developed over its short history until 1968, the themes of "settlement", "siege mentality", "penal laws" and "deprivation" were clearly evident. But in so evolving, Northern Ireland could not establish either the means or the conditions for an inclusive, reconciled or even a permanently stable society. On the contrary, both in the manner of its inception and of its evolution, the seeds of its own destruction were gradually ripening. [Farren & Mulvihill, 2000, p. 20]

This destruction became acted out in the idealization of oppressive practices in housing and employment. For the Protestant establishment "might was right", and this was manifested in the self-justified actions of putting Catholics in their place. Here, we can also draw on the behaviour of crowds or large groups to explain how destructiveness or the death instinct becomes so valued that anything is possible. It was Freud who brought our attention to the power of large groups in his text "Group psychology and the analysis of the ego" (1921). He described how the frenzy of the crowd or mass movement projects on the leader characteristics of their superego, or death instinct, which frees them from rational humanistic thinking and behaviour. Through mutual identification, there emerges a common cause or common fight either to rid the crowd/society of evil or to put people in their place. Kernberg adds:

In fact, it is striking how intensely aggression is activated in small groups, in large groups and in mass movements (however short lived or enduring they may be) enabling individuals to behave in violent ways that would be unthinkable for them under ordinary life circumstances structured by ordinary status–role relationships. In other words, the normal process of socialisation in the family; the elaboration, sublimation, repression and reaction formations dealing with primitive aggression; the normal tolerance of ambivalence with a corresponding dominance of love over hatred; the normal acknowledgement of aggression with efforts towards its rational and conscious control all seem to get lost almost instantaneously under certain conditions of group functioning. (Kernberg, 2003a, p. 686]

So, depriving ordinary Catholic people of housing and passing laws to devalue and marginalize ordinary people can easily be justified through the psychology of mass movement, which itself can so easily justify the act of destroying or putting down others.

Idealizaton of institutions

As stated earlier, Northern Ireland is a very status conscious society. Academic, professional, and religious institutions tend to be idealized. Civic leaders can also perpetuate this idealization by demanding that their flock project only good parts of themselves. Intelligence, competence, and spiritual thought is sucked up by dysfunctional leaders to deal with their own emotional inadequacies.

The two universities in Northern Ireland compete viciously to be the best and most favoured academic child. Both are guilty of academic superiority complex, where they project their failings into non-academic people. In reality, neither is in the "Russell Group" of universities, as the top academic institutions in the UK are defined, despite having recently improved their research and teaching quality ratings. Both fail to communicate this fact to the Northern Ireland public. Academics from both institutions will actively engage in academic put-downs with ordinary souls in the false belief that they are better. In fact, true excellence in academia is characterized by the wise saying "the more you know, the less you know".

Professional organizations are guilty of a similar crime. Doctors, lawyers, and associated professions believe they are of a higher human race. Again, internal feelings of inadequacy are projected on to and into lesser souls. This strict external hierarchy mirrors the internal world. A patient said:

> My father was a doctor. Good in the head and weak in the heart. He got the usual acclaims from his patients and colleagues. All I wanted was his affection and acceptance. He couldn't show it. He felt he was above that.

Again, this translates into day-to-day human relations. In my experience the emotionally distant professionals are not only the most difficult to reach (Joseph, 1989) but they are also the most unhappy. Inner emptiness is filled by "feel good" projections from others and projecting into others their inferiority. Institutional idealization confirms this pathological process.

This group behaviour is similar to the previous comments made in this chapter about religion and fundamentalism. Fundamentalism exists in every organization, whether it is religious, political, or professional, and has been well known within the history of psychoanalysis and psychotherapy. The essential feature of how organizations maintain this pseudo-cohesiveness is by projecting outwards their bad and inadequate feelings. This, of course, becomes institutionalized and then is embedded in the culture of the organization as "normal behaviour". Ordinary humanity and human courtesies are sacrificed in the face of this puritanical state of mind, which is felt to protect the institution from bad people and emotional toxins and infections. As is described in the final paragraph of this chapter, terrorism is not the monopoly of terrorist military groups, particularly within a troubled mind society. Institutional fundamentalism will use all of its powers to rid itself of bad feelings, which are perceived to be a threat to its own goodness.

This permeation of primitive regressive forces has been noticed by the work of Vamik Volkan in his psychoanalytic work in areas of political conflict.

> It is readily evident that conflicts involving large group identities have made and continue to make traditional diplomatic relations

and conflict resolution nearly impossible in parts of Africa, Europe, Transcausasia, the Middle East and practically every other region. The withdrawal of colonial powers from India and Africa, and the collapse of the Soviet system, brought us bloodshed and malignant massive behaviours, mostly within states, that were closely related to issues of large-group identity. In the former Yugoslavia, for example, Serbs, Croats and Bosnians re-asserted their large-group identity and soon became involved in a violent process of defining themselves and demonizing others. [Volkan, 1999, p. 462]

Volkan quotes the particular work of the psychoanalyst Cullberg-Weston (1997) in Yugoslavia when he writes:

[In Yugoslavia] we found a strong tendency toward splitting. Images were split into good/bad and into we/them categories. Almost everyone idealised their own ethnic group and demonized others. . . . The black and white thinking was further encouraged by nationalistic leaders who actively played on group antipathy, using propaganda aimed at creating fear, rage and insecurity about people's safety. [*ibid.*, p. 463]

It is important to recognize that when a society is troubled, the very institutions that run society will mimic the same regressive features of the wider society. This is also a critical element in the formula for change to the depressive position. As stated several times in this text, we cannot project all the power into politicians. The very way we run our institutions is tainted by the malignancy of the paranoid–schizoid position, where primitive splitting is deemed normal. Institutionalized psychological cleansing has to stop to put a halt to primitive regressive object relations that will only perpetuate the cycle of psychic violence.

Middle-class terrorism

The central dynamic of terrorism is to strike fear, via projective identification, into others. In Northern Ireland, and elsewhere, this is usually associated with working-class paramilitary groups. However, striking fear into the hearts and minds of others is a central characteristic of paranoid–schizoid functioning and is rampant in everyday life when a society is exposed to much death and destruction. Again, Kernberg highlights the emotional aspect of this particular object relation when he writes:

> The primary objective of terrorism is the production of terror, that is, a paralyzing, dis-organising sense of dread that spreads among the enemy, destabilizing and eventually de-legitimizing the enemy's social structure, way of living and leadership. . . . By projective identification, the terrorist's dread is his own ruthless destruction by the enemy, so that death becomes an essential aspect of the terrorist's mental world. [Kernberg, 2003b, p. 958]

Of course, to create terror in others there has to be an internalization of terrorist experience, which can occur either directly, or indirectly through the media. Direct experience of terror may not be confined to witnessing particular terrorist events, but can also occur in family, work, and other settings. If terror is seen as the normal way of conducting human relationships then inevitably this becomes acted out in day-to-day relationships. Brunet and Casoni (1991) analyse this further by digging deep into the internal world of the terrorist who is spreading fear through intimidation

> In the present essay, the hypothesis is that the dynamics of the internal world in witnessing of terrorist acts, necessarily reflect, for the most part, the intra-psychic phenomena which seem to be going on within terrorists themselves. To elaborate: a person who has committed or who has provoked a destructive and violent act has also experienced . . . the same phenomena of identification with the victims. [Brunet & Casoni, 1991, p. 9]

In other words, terrorists contain within their own minds experiences of terror and fear which they then project on to others. Experiencing terrorism is omnipresent, whereby fear and intimidation are the currency of everyday human relations. In Northern Ireland, as in any society afflicted by terror, this is endemic.

The middle classes in Northern Ireland live prosperous lives, visibly untroubled by terrorist events. As detailed in Chapter One, the acting out of middle-class sectarianism has been through the allocation of jobs reflecting skewed employment patterns favouring Protestants. My thesis is that this has been a false safety, as

unconsciously the day-to-day relations of these apparently sheltered people have taken on the characteristics of the terrorists they
see in the media.

I have reported elsewhere (Rice & Kapur, 2002) my own professional experiences of being terrorized to act in a certain way "or
else". Threat overtakes thought and thus there is little hope of
depressive position functioning. Coupling is inevitably characterized by a wish to dominate and thus strike fear into the other
person, who inevitably is in a more subordinate and inferior position. Another example from my own experience as Chief Execu-
tive/Director of a charity in the voluntary sector highlights this.
The statutory sector, representing mental health hospitals and
community organizations are inevitably in a "top-dog" position,
as they are the purchasers and we are the providers. This leads to a
projection of inadequacy into the voluntary sector which, in fact,
provides the same public service free of charge to people with
mental health problems. In a troubled mind, people can automatically re-enact terrorist object relations where they see an opportunity to abuse power.

In this terrorist state of mind, a human ideology is clearly absent
(Kernberg, 2003a) and so there is a regression to part-object relationships. Again, we have to ask the question; is it a coincidence
that we have the highest number of industrial tribunals and rates
of alcoholism in the UK, or does this reflect an acting out of aggressive terrorist human relations in the middle-classes? No one can be
immune to the effects of terror.

Kernberg (2003b), in writing about the containment of terrorism,
puts the cure into social, political, and military interventions.
However, this reflects how fear and intimidation are manifested in
day-to-day human relations. A "bottom-up" approach, where leaders and people in enemy roles cease to control others by fear, can
surely have only a positive impact on the breeding grounds and
thus support terrorist activities. It may be only with the creation of
a whole-object humanistic ideology across all of society that the
real cure for terrorism will be found. When examining the life
stories of both Republican and Loyalist terrorists, it is clear that
their "states of mind" began to change only when they realized that
their victims were human beings. Only then can thought replace
threat. As Collins (2001) wrote: "I fought to curb what I saw as my

"weakness", namely, my readiness to see my victims as ordinary human beings and their deaths as deserving sympathy."

Conclusion

For a society to become less troubled, individuals have to re-own their authority. Authority located in a leader creates an infantile dependence. Good experiences of authority must also occur, which will inhibit the primitive wish to overthrow the leader. Fight–flight responses have to be replaced by focusing and thinking about issues that are propelling groups to act in such destructive ways. For the future:

- civic leaders and those in leadership roles have to pay serious attention to giving good experiences of authority that is free from corruption and favouritism;
- in the words of the philosopher, Jiddu Krishnamurti,

  You don't have to believe what I say—far from it. If you believe what I say, then it is your misery not mine; then you will use me as another authority, and therefore take shelter and comfort . . . to have a Master in India, or in some mountain far away from your daily life is very convenient, very encouraging because then you can say, "well, I'll like him in my next life". [Krishnamurti, 1983, p. 73]

- members of groups, institutions and organizations have to take responsibility for their destructive impulses to undermine and overthrow the leader.

Leaders and group followers projecting inadequate and aggressive aspects of themselves on to others can only perpetuate trauma. Everyone has to take responsibility to relate differently.

CHAPTER SIX

Responding to the violence of the Troubles: the role of professionals and other care-givers

Introduction

In previous chapters we have argued that substantive parts of Northern Irish society have been traumatized by violence, whether this is at individual, group, or structural levels. It is pertinent, therefore, to ask whether there are mechanisms available to help those who have suffered and for those who support people who have been traumatized. This chapter reviews the historical development of services for people affected by the Troubles and assesses what impact the violence has had on professionals. What emerges is a story of piecemeal service delivery, shaped by the social divisions in Northern Ireland, failures in political processes, and the operation of professional ideologies that fostered limited opportunities for Troubles-related interventions. The problematic issue of victimhood and current plans by the devolved assembly to deliver more appropriate help to people who have suffered as a consequence of the Troubles are discussed. In the concluding sections of the chapter we use object relations theory to explain and interpret some of the problematic scenarios that have been created by thirty years of political violence.

An historical overview

In examining how health and social care professionals have responded to the political violence of the last thirty years, it is essential to analyse critically the development of state and welfare agencies in Northern Ireland. At many times during the last three decades the sheer scale of social disruption caused by intercommunal and state violence created the conditions in which individual professionals and their agencies were forced to abandon traditional methods and discourses. For example, when the current Troubles exploded on the streets of Northern Ireland in the late 1960s, existing services were unable to cope with the enormous levels of unmet social needs. In health care settings, doctors and nurses were faced with the aftermath of widespread bombings and shootings which left thousands of people physically injured and psychologically scarred. Social care staff were required to be flexible about their use of social assistance and sometimes obliged to negotiate access to communities through paramilitary groups. These sudden changes in the way professionals carried out their work profoundly affected agencies that, hitherto, had delivered conventional services to a relatively small region within the UK (Darby & Williamson, 1978). This sense of chaos, and the subsequent challenges to existing systems of health and social care, suggests that, for those who suffered as a result of such violence, they could only expect at best a haphazard response to their situation.

Although there are many possible reasons for such gaps between need and service delivery, a crucial explanatory factor was the way in which the state administered and delivered health and social care in the decades that followed the outbreak of the present Troubles. A defining moment in the development of health and social welfare services in Northern Ireland followed the decision in 1972 to introduce Direct Rule by the central government in Westminster. The "integrated service", unique in the context of the UK in that most professional groups involved in the delivery of health and social welfare are employed within the same organization, was established in 1973. The reorganization of services allowed policy-makers and professionals to plan and deliver health and social welfare services relatively free from local political demands.

Because the introduction of the service coincided with a crisis in the state, there are competing views on how beneficial this policy has been. This policy shift can be viewed either as an attempt to resolve long-standing problems of discrimination and sectarianism in the absence of social and political consensus between the "two communities", or as a method of containing and managing a conflict in which the state had a part to play. It has been argued, for example, that the widespread use of quasi-autonomous governmental and non-governmental agencies in Northern Ireland since Direct Rule was part of a rational strategy to remove power from a discredited local political system and place it in the hands of a small group of ministers, their civil servants, and non-discriminatory professionals. (Birrell & Murie, 1980). A more critical appraisal of the rationale for Direct Rule suggests that central government used these mechanisms to at best manage, rather than resolve, the conflict (O'Dowd *et al.*, 1980). Although there may have been some benefits in terms of conventional service delivery (Campbell & McLaughlin, 2000) the integrated service, however, was less effective in addressing the needs of people traumatized by violence. Campbell & Pinkerton (1997) and Pinkerton and Campbell (2002) have challenged the underlying assumption that staff could in fact make professional judgements somehow detached from experiences of living in such a conflictual society. Inevitably, political and social factors have influenced practice. One of the consequences of the government's project to distance state welfare bureaucracies from local communities was that professionals and agencies were often unsure of how and when to intervene when traumatic incidents occurred.

This critique of the state can be helpful in explaining why most health and social care professionals who, throughout this period, were trained to deal with apolitical issues in an efficient way, are poorly equipped to deal with their own, as well as their clients', feelings about past and present conflict. For example, the effect of sectarianism helped to enforce a collective silence about potentially dangerous political and social agendas, and prevent opportunities for reconciliation in the field of social work in Northern Ireland (Smyth & Campbell, 1996; Traynor, 1998; Campbell & Healey, 1999). Other professional groups have barely acknowledged the impact of the conflict on their practice or have rarely had the opportunity to speak about how the violence has affected them (Smyth *et al.*, 2001). The consequence of these sets of circumstances is that professionals in health and social care fields tend to attach great importance to "normal" ways of functioning in this abnormal social and political context. This may be viewed as a way of distancing themselves from painful stories that clients sometimes disclose. Other aspects of service delivery reflect other features of a society that is deeply divided. For example, young people and adults have been often been admitted to psychiatric hospitals in psychologically distressed states, fleeing from paramilitary or security force threats. In this respect the hospital becomes an asylum, in its literal sense (Campbell & Healey, 1999).

In the two decades that followed the start of the Troubles, policy-makers and practitioners were generally ill-equipped to deal with traumatic incidents when they occurred. In fact, the first concerted attempt to deliver a comprehensive service in this area followed a civil incident. This was initiated as a result of the crash of an aeroplane carrying people from London to Belfast, nearly two decades after Bloody Sunday (Gibson, 1996), rather than any of the earlier Troubles-related incidents of the previous decades. During the period of Direct Rule, the failure of politics and security policies reinforced the perception of a society in stasis, with little opportunity for dialogue and conflict resolution. It would be wrong, however, to assume that, as a consequence of this vacuum, professionals and organizations always delivered trauma-related services randomly. The effect of much policy and practice was to render some groups apparently less deserving of services than others; the construction of a range of victimologies took place. For example, families of paramilitaries and communities that supported them, and others who had suffered because of their activity as part of a social movement against the state, were more likely to avoid statutory services and, instead, seek to organize informal mechanisms of support. The growth in prisoner and ex-prisoner support groups over the years reflects this phenomenon. On the other hand, security service members and their families tended to fall back on discreet forms of health and social welfare services, located outside, or hidden within, mainstream organizations, often for reasons of personal safety (Hayes & Campbell, 2000). For the great majority of the population trauma-based services were at best *ad hoc* and uneven. These are what (Bloomfield, 1998: p. 30) described as "the many 'little people' caught up in violence, often in relatively isolated incidents too soon forgotten outside the immediate family".

It is only now, nearly a decade after the first loyalist and republican paramilitary cease-fires in 1994, that policies and services for victims of the Troubles are being developed in a more comprehensive fashion. During this time a number of significant events, finally leading to the establishment of the Northern Ireland Assembly and Executive, have allowed for some reflection on past violence and the consideration of new ways of dealing with trauma (McGarry, 2001; Morrissey & Smyth, 2002). Growing interest in researching the affects of the Troubles implies that it is only in recent years, using the space offered during conflict resolution, that a well of previously unmet emotional and psychological need has emerged. One event in the recent past has, understandably become the focus of much attention in terms of policy in this area. On 28 August 1998, a bomb planted in the town of Omagh killed twenty-eight people and two unborn children. Another person was to die later. As the largest number of deaths caused by any violent incident in the previous years of the Troubles, the Omagh bombing left an indelible impression on local, national and international opinion, coming as it did in the midst of the peace process and following the political settlement described in the Belfast Agreement (NIO, 1998a). The response of services at the time, and in the aftermath of such a major traumatic incident, also suggested that workers were better equipped and more prepared for the consequent multi-layered problems faced by families and the community than they might have been in the past. This is not to say, however, that problems still remain for professionals in addressing their own painful emotions and memories of the past (Kapur, 2001). In addition, the subsequent funding for a trauma centre, which was set up to deal with the sequelae of the Omagh bombing, has brought to light the problems of making difficult choices about the competing needs of other groups and geographical locations in Northern Ireland (Morrissey & Smyth, 2002, pp.14–15; Smyth et al., 2001).

A fundamental, continuous problem to be resolved for citizens and policy-makers alike is the issue of how we define "victimhood". Baseline audits can produce stark "facts" with which to begin, although most commentators recognized the need to avoid establishing a hierarchy of victimhood, as though suffering can be neatly packaged and measured. For example, Smyth and Hamilton (2003) surveyed the numbers of those who have died during the Troubles. They found that, of the 3,601 people who died between 1969 and 2001, some groups were more represented than others in the statistics.

● Most fatalities occurred between 1971 and 1976 (over 50% of all deaths).
● The main perpetrators have been paramilitary groups (80%).
● Republican groups were responsible for 55.7% and Loyalist for 27.4% of all deaths.
● All security forces were responsible for 10% of deaths.
● 91% of all those killed were male.
● Those in their twenties and thirties were most affected (over 50%).
● More Catholics than Protestants have been victims.
● The IRA was responsible for 85% of all killings by Republicans.
● Republicans, Loyalist and Protestant paramilitaries were responsible for a significant number of Catholic deaths.
● Almost all security force deaths were caused by Republicans.
● Across all groups responsible for deaths, the largest category of victims was civilian.

In some ways, these problems are at least recognized and beginning to be considered. On the first page of the Good Friday Agreement there is an explicit acknowledgement of the need to reorganize services and to find ways of dealing with the legacy of the past. Two reports (Department of Health & Social Services (Northern Ireland) (DHSS(NI)), 1998; Bloomfield, 1998) recognized the limitations of past services provided to those who have suffered, and recommend that:

● there should be recognition of all individuals and groups who have suffered;
● welfare and legal services should be sensitive to the needs of those who have suffered;
● the voluntary and community sectors should be better supported;

- statutory agencies should organize a comprehensive system of crisis teams;
- professional psychology and counselling services should be expanded and accredited;
- consideration should be given to a form of permanent memorial to victims;
- adequate systems of compensation should be examined and arranged.

In the last few years the Northern Ireland Office, the Office of the First and Deputy First Minister, other departments at Stormont, and a range of voluntary agencies have initiated a number of projects associated with victims' needs. What has materialized from this activity is the realization of the breadth of Troubles-related problems to be dealt with, and the range and intensity of views on how to proceed. For example, at one level, there is a sense that some people have "objectively" suffered more than others during the Troubles, in terms of physical, psychological, social, and economic tragedy (Hamber, 1998), and yet at the same time it is difficult to measure one person's grief against another's. As an acknowledgement of the problems of achieving a universal definition, and perhaps to avoid rhetorical battles about victimhood, the government has adopted the following definition:

> The surviving physically and psychologically injured of violent, conflict related incidents and those close relatives or partners who care for them, along with those close relatives or partners who mourn their dead. [Office of the First and Deputy First Minister, 2002, p. 1]

The report, *Reshape, Rebuild, Achieve* (Office of the First and Deputy First Minister, 2002), identifies a wide range of policies and strategies to address the needs of people who have been traumatized, including: the improvement of service delivery; ensuring cross-departmental responsiveness; encouraging interorganizational working; and establishing a variety of funding mechanisms to meet the diverse needs of victims and victims' groups. The report, in listing the growing range of organizations involved in helping in Troubles-related fields, highlights a greater role for the voluntary and community sectors in this form of provision. The Department of Health, Social Services and Public Safety (DHSSPS) has recently published a report on a review of counselling in Northern Ireland, part of which seeks to improve practice, education, and training for those professionals who may be dealing with the needs of victims (DHSSPS, 2002a). To date, around £15 m over a period of a recent years has been spent by central government on a range of victims'/survivors' issues.

The question remains as to whether Northern Irish society is currently willing or prepared to find some common ground to resolve the complex issues of blame, guilt, and reparation that flow from the many traumatic incidents which have occurred during the Troubles (Morrissey & Smyth, 2002). As in other areas of intense social and political violence around the world (Hamber, 1998; Hamber *et al.*, 2000), the process of conflict resolution in Northern Ireland appears to have a long way to go before a sense of common trust emerges that might allow the resolution of these issues. In some ways the beginnings of this process has been acknowledged through the government's recognition of the Healing Through Remembering project, which collated 108 submissions about how the process of remembering "may address the legacy of the conflict in and about Northern Ireland" (DHSSPS, 2002b, p. ii). As a result of this consultation process, six detailed recommendations were made: to develop networks of storytelling; to build an archive of narratives or testimonies about the conflict; to establish an annual day of reflection; to construct a living memorial museum; to find ways of encouraging all those involved in the conflict to acknowledge their responsibilities for political violence; and the examination of the possibility of creating a unique truth recovery process.

Object relations theory and helping the professionals

The conclusion which can be drawn from this history of policy practice is that different mechanisms and approaches are needed to deal with the diversity of social and emotional need that has arisen because of the troubles in Northern Ireland. We believe that the application of object relations theory to some of these phenomena may help us to understand ways of resolving such trauma. For example, the development of policies and investment of resources alone will not necessarily deal with deeper, internal effects of trauma; professionals themselves may not be equipped to cope with the intensity of such profound stories as told by their clients. The process of healing is complex and multi-faceted, helpers need help to understand how this may affect them. Wilson (1989), for example, lists the main reactions of the psychotherapist to traumatic story telling:

- emotional intensity and distress;
- fear;
- anxiety and bystander guilt;
- empathic distress;
- psychic numbing and avoidance reactions;
- over-identification with the victim.

These themes will now be used to explore how the troubles may have affected professionals in Northern Ireland, using the conceptual framework outlined in Chapter Two.

Emotional intensity and distress

Many people identify with the troubles. Both Protestants and Catholics see, time and time again, their own side being traumatized. This gives rise to an emotional intensity that affects day-to-day states of mind. Outrage at perceived injustice, along with a wish for revenge, dominates in this troubled state of mind. Revenge and retaliation become the language of everyday discourse. What is more worrying is that this permeates into day-to-day human relations conflicts, thus making entry to the depressive position all the more difficult. Containment of toxic projective processes is essential for the professional to retain his or her balance. Personal reports from mental health professionals working in north and west Belfast, the areas where most terrorist incidents and murders have taken place, testify to the amount of distress requiring containment.

> At the beginning of the Troubles I was involved in seeing all these poor children etc in the Royal [the local hospital, Royal Victoria Hospital] . . . it was very hard, very stressful from my point of view, and the people I worked with.

And

> I was overwhelmed with stress, because it could be interpreted as
> weakness, and you're not coping with your job therefore you're not
> up to it. [Smyth *et al.*, 2001, pp. 122–123]

The key element of containment is to recognize the emotional
impact of particular events on your state of mind. In particular,
unless negative projections are acknowledged and detoxified, the
individual suffers considerable intensity of feelings and distress.
Yet professionally and publicly, these reactions often go unrecognized. In failing to acknowledge the effects of these emotional reactions, could it be that the poor state of health in Northern Ireland
represents a somatization of years of exposure to the intense
emotional effects of the Troubles?

• Are the high rates of heart attack a result of a troubled mind
  creating Type A troubled mind personalities that are hostile,
  aggressive, and strict in personal object relations?
• Do the high ranges of psychosomatic disorders such as gastro-
  intestinal problems and related disorders such as diabetes
  indicate a high prevalence of troubled minds where there is
  a somatic conversion of intense emotions unconsciously
  absorbed through exposure to the Troubles?
• Are the high rates of tranquillizers and axiolyotic prescription
  (75% higher than Great Britain) and anti-depressants (37%
  higher than Great Britain) reflecting an emotional distress
  caused by so much exposure to hatred and violence?
• Do the low rates of breast-feeding indicate a reluctance to
  acknowledge softer maternal containment and indicate the
  absence of this positive emotional experience in everyday
  life?

All of these questions, and many more, could only be answered
through empirical research. However, any human being exposed
to such troubles can only but naturally respond with emotional
intensity and distress which, if unrecognized, causes major difficulties.

Anxiety

Persecutory anxiety is at the heart of paranoid–schizoid functioning. Exposure to unpredictable terrorist attacks leaves people with a deep fear that it may happen again. Wilson describes this counter-transference reaction in therapists as follows:

> Closely related to anger counter-transference issues are reactions of fear in the therapist, which usually stems from two sources. Firstly, many traumatized persons are angry to the point of rage and homicidal fantasies of retaliation and "payback". The intensity of the anger and rage is so pronounced that it frightens some therapists who are not accustomed to such reactions. The affective intensity of the client may elicit fear responses in the therapist . . . the affective intensity of rage actually corresponds to the level of "subjective vulnerability". Thus counter-transference feelings of fear and vulnerability are also closely related to one another. This then, is the second source of fear, which grows out of the empathic awareness that victimization can lead to states of helplessness, belittlement, humiliation, degradation and the destruction of will. [Wilson, 1989, p. 206]

Here, we have two major personal reactions, noticeable in therapists, which affect anyone exposed to hostility. A great deal of fear and anxiety is carried around unconsciously in troubled minds, and phantasies of retaliation are part and parcel of the destructive processes within the paranoid–schizoid position. "Our time will come" or in Irish, "*Tiochfadh ar la*" is a phrase carried around in the mind of many Catholics who look forward to the time when old scores will be settled. What is so evident in day-to-day disclosure in Northern Ireland is how these strong feelings are lurking onmipresently beneath the surface. For Catholics it is the fear of being dominated by the external objects of Unionism. For Protestants it is the fear of being dominated by the external object of Nationalist Republicanism. Of course, both fears carry their own vulnerabilities. It is only when such vulnerabilities can be addressed that more depressive position functioning take place. A more positive outcome can then be achieved, one that takes everyone into account with no exploitation of anyone's vulnerabilities by either side, so reducing levels of persecutory anxiety.

An example of the massive anxiety carried around in the mind of someone affected by the Troubles is described in this woman's nightmares:

> To this day I have nighmares, and I mean terrible, terrible night-mares. It used to be every night screaming, yelling. I was lucky whenever I had Gail here with me: she would come in and waken me. If there's nobody there to waken you, you have to scream and yell and you hurt yourself. I told mummy and daddy that if ever I got found dead in bed it'll be because of a nightmare, because of the pain across my chest and down my arms with me screaming, trying to get myself woke. Its okay whenever there is someone there to waken you, you don't yell as long. During the day you have plenty to do, you can pass yourself, but whenever your head hits the pillow it's all going through you're [sic] mind again: and you're thinking about what you would do to the killers. (HURT Victims' Support Group, 2001, p. 30]

Anxiety and bystander guilt

Many people who witness a traumatic event and experience great anxiety and feel unable to do anything about it; professionals who try to help can also be profoundly affected. A social worker in a troubled area of Belfast describes the following experience.

> Just a few months ago a person I work with was given a punish-ment beating ... he was literally left for dead. It's the worst I've ever come across. His younger brother has since been threatened. I was out with the family last week and the stress on the Mother was horrendous. I just felt she was at breaking point. And they've put in for a housing transfer which was a big decision, because they've lived in this area all their lives, but felt they needed to move out of it. The Housing Executive were saying to me, even though they are A1 priority, it will be up to two years, and they'll be lucky if in two years we have found somewhere for this family. And I came off the phone and I, first of all, felt like crying. Because this family have been through the mill when it comes to the Troubles ... and then I felt anger. And I think I was tuning in a bit to what you were saying [other colleague] when you felt [when] you were in the car

that day and you couldn't get past, and it was part of the stress of working is the sheer frustration, you've no impact on being able to stop what happened to that young fella, I couldn't influence the paramilitaries in his area of the community. [Smyth *et al.*, 2001, p. 63]

Either this bystander guilt can be transformed into reparative guilt, where there is a wish to repair what has been destroyed, or there emerges a persecutory guilt where helplessness is transformed into self-persecution. The sign of a productive, helping relationship in these circumstances is where professionals can engage with clients in working through these processes. Reparative acts are taking place, as described earlier, in the many actions of statutory, voluntary, and community groups working with victim and survivors of the Troubles. The Troubled Mind Project (Kapur, 2002) is an attempt to do this by providing group psychotherapy for people traumatized by the troubles. This act of reparation applies a form of psychological treatment, group psychotherapy, that hitherto has really only been applied to the middle-classes in this society. Psychotherapy and psychoanalysis has been mainly for the chosen few in a highly class-ridden society. The alternative to this reparative action is either persecutory guilt or a schizoid detachment from the distress we have seen in others.

Empathic distress

Wilson describes this phenomenon as:

A general category of counter-transference reactions, including states of sadness, grief, dread, horror, disgust, shame, or revulsion at what has been disclosed in the trauma story. Sadness and grief reactions in the therapist are natural products of empathic listening but may also be manifestations of issues of personal loss and prolonged grief responses. Reactions of dread, horror, disgust, revulsion and shame are also experienced by clinicians working with traumatized individuals. It is important to remember that traumatic stressors include such events as rape, torture, war atrocity (e.g. mutilation) disfiguring injuries, and burns, as well as exposure to grotesque situations. [Wilson, 1989, p. 207]

Exposure to terror and persecution stirs up deep anxieties in all of us. Kleinian psychoanalysis highlights the depth of these troubling personal reactions by identifying the existence of profound anxieties within the paranoid–schizoid position. Mitrani points to the work of Tustin in directing our attention to this.

> Tustin was perhaps most widely appreciated for her evocative descriptions of some of the most elemental human terrors above and active in each of us, as well as those specialized protective forms that ordinary people create in order to survive. Among those she noted the sensations of mutiliation, of spilling and faking, of dissolving and evaporating, which characterize what she called the terrors of two-ness. She then traced the problem of psychogenic autism to the troubled nature of the earliest relationship between mother and nursing. [Mitrani, 2001, p. 33]

It would appear that the mechanisms of Northern Irish society have failed to provide a good-enough maternal container for the persecutory and anniliatory anxieties of its citizens. It is also important, however, to avoid victim-blaming, as though we in this part of the world have to live, or die, by our own faults. The analysis can be extended to explain relationships within these islands and the wider international community. For example, Northern Irish society, it might be asserted, has been at the receiving end of poor maternal containment from its parental neighbours, Britain and Ireland, and has thus been unable to develop supportive mechanisms of its own. The result is a reinforcement of persecutory anxieties through the witnessing of the horrors of murder and violence and a significant lack of good experiences or good objects that can detoxify such experiences. Movement to the depressive position, where persecutory anxieties can be replaced by safety and trust, places an onus on everyone, particularly those in professional and political authority, to be better containers for the toxicity of a troubled mind.

This involves a collective societal action to provide more good than bad experiences in everyday life. With so many negative projective processes creating a toxic environment of hate and envy in everyday human relations, there emerges an onus on individuals and institutions to "make good" what has been "torn asunder" through real and phantasized acts of destruction. Thought and concern have to slowly replace action and selfishness for true depressive position functioning to flourish.

Psychic numbing and avoidance

Any container overloaded with anxiety has its limits. When the violence and hostility projected into the individual professional or layperson becomes too much there is a schizoid or cutting-off reaction. Mitrani describes this as stirring up much earlier and deeper anxieties and refers to the work of Wittenberg (1997) when she writes:

> She [Wittenberg] identified a pattern wherein babies who are born highly sensitive and intelligent, and with a great lust for life and beauty, are often overwhelmed with depressive anxiety when their perception of a lively, responsive and caring object (this is, the mindful breast) failed to materialise. While holding themselves responsible for this disturbance in the Mother, they attempt to project her omnipotently. However, the failure of such attempts triggers a shift in the ordinary human object to a "hard object" that is often manifested in some obsessional activity used as an escape from the terror of hopelessness and death. (Mitrani, 2001, p. 36]

This "hard object" concept refers also to the hard man profile discussed in Chapter Three. Individuals inure themselves to trauma by toughening up. In Kleinian language, a schizoid, split-off relationship exists with the world and people are treated as part-objects, numbers, rather than real people.

For so many years people in Northern Ireland exposed to distress have dealt with trauma through distancing and schizoid functioning. This is a natural reaction to threat, but repeated exposure to violence leads to an emotional withdrawal where "hard" states of mind are developed to manage unbearable persecutory and negative feelings. A family whose members have suffered from the Troubles report their experience of numbing.

> The media's habit of using footage of past murders was something which caused a great deal of upset. I know one of the things that

hits Thelma and Pearl very hard, is that every time there's an article or a documentary on TV their two sons are shown lying dead on the pavement. Yes, the media's habit of using footage of past murders has caused a great deal of upset to those families concerned. You may be walking into the living room and are caught unawares. And when you see your son on TV lying dead you reach for the tablet bottle again. You just feel numb all over - no-one knows just what goes through you at that moment. It is like a bad dream. But in your heart you know that it is true. David will not walk through that door ever again, no kiss on the cheek, or "how are you, mum?". He was a good son and people on both sides knew that he and John Graham were two good community Police Officers who did their job well. [HURT Victims' Support Group, 2001, p. 6]

Over-identification

Often professionals can move out of their normal professional, objective reactions to traumatic situations. This over-identification can lead to significant problems. Wilson outlines these as follows:

... the therapist may over-identify with the victim out of a sensitive and deep empathic understanding of how the person was
psychically injured by the trauma. This level of empathic caring
may then lead to being overly committed to helping the patient,
which, in turn, may potentially facilitate excessive dependency and
over-idealisation of the therapist. [Wilson, 1989, p. 210]

When the identification is too great, professionals can unwit-tingly create an infantile dependency with the patient that is seen as treating the psychic distress. As Northern Ireland is a small place (a population of less than 1.7 million) it may be that the professional either knows the people involved in the terrorist incident or has someone close to them that has experienced a similar event. The hope is that, if the professional intensely involves themselves with the patient, alleviation of distress will occur. Here, there is a cure by proxy, what has been described as a "transference cure". An over-dependency addresses the distress but when the professional leaves the distress returns. Attention must be paid to the complexity of counter-transference reactions to ensure that the professional does not act out his or her own anxieties, so disrupting the helping relationship/alliance and leading to a false and only transient change.

Conclusion

In this chapter we have described the development of the services for people who have been traumatized by the troubles in Northern Ireland. This is a problematic story that is still to be completed. In recent years attempts have been made to redress the many problems created by political violence, and services to victims and survivors have improved. But we have argued that many of the deep-seated worries and anxieties faced by professionals and their clients remain unresolved. The interpretations, using object relations theory, that conclude this chapter may help us in understanding why some professionals remain trapped in organizations and practise discourses that often do not deal with underlying psychic issues. In the concluding chapter we discuss ways in which we believe individuals, professionals, and wider society can deal with such issues.

CHAPTER SEVEN

Conclusion: the way forward

I n this book we have highlighted the internal personality factors that are an integral part of a troubled state of mind, as well as emphasizing conditions that perpetuate the aggressive and violent style of human relatedness which so often happens in Northern Ireland. So what is the cure or solution? Is it purely internal or does personal responsibility for change have to be coupled with changes in the external world? In this final chapter we lay particular emphasis on the psychoanalytic processes that have to be put in place for the ordinary citizen to achieve a more peaceful state of mind. We will also comment on the social and political processes that need to occur in tandem with a change in the internal world to maximize the possibility of real peace.

Psychoanalytic ideas

In summarizing the conditions for change to take place Kernberg writes:

> From a psychoanalytic perspective, finally, the question may be raised: what are the possibilities of a terrorist to escape the terrorist

system and return to a condition of normality that resolves the personal regression, the split-off aggression and the submersion in a fundamentalist ideology? Obviously, this depends on the personal psychopathology of the terrorist, the extent to which paranoid personality dispositions that foster entrance into a paranoid group psychology are not part of a more malignant narcissism, and are not accompanied by significant anti-social features. Relative maintenance of an ordinary capacity for human empathy and identification with ethical values may permit some terrorists to leave their system once its basic sadism, cruelty, irrationality and humanity become obvious to them. We certainly have examples of this in political leaders who emerged from an early identification with a terrorist group such as in the case of Menachem Begin, in Israel, eventually Prime Minister in Israel, and Joska Fischer, eventually Foreign Secretary of the German Federal Republic. [Kernberg, 2003b, p. 966]

With the creation of the local assembly we have certainly seen examples of where people with a "terrorist" history have been able to activate depressive position functioning and perform tasks that are creative, and for the good of the whole population. We review the processes involved for this change to occur and in so doing highlight the inherent difficulties in moving out of paranoid–schizoid functioning into a more human approach to everyday relationships.

Identity

As mentioned in previous chapters, there is a tremendous identity or emotional charge gained from possessing a violent identity. The autobiographies of the Republican (Collins, 1997) and Loyalist (Sinnerton, 2002; Stone, 2003) paramilitaries highlight how psychological strength is gained from an idealization of violence and a "hard man" approach to conflict. The same could be said for those involved in state terror in Northern Ireland. This "hard man" mentality is pervasive across many individuals, groups, and institutions who have been involved in the conflict of the past thirty years.

It is truly within the paranoid–schizoid position that this psychic violence is so keenly felt and idealized. This hints at a severe disruption to containment either by the societal mother or much earlier in the psychological life of people. The mutually reinforcing nature of paranoid–schizoid makes it extremely difficult to find an escape from this predominately aggressive style of human relations. The internal change is massive. Clinically, this is best summarized by the work of Rosenfeld.

> The destructive omnipotent way of living like Simon often appears highly organised, as if one were dealing with a powerful gang dominated by a leader, who controls all the members of the gang to see that they support one another in making the criminal destructive work more effective and powerful. However, the narcissistic organisation not only increases the strength of the destructive narcissism, and the deadly force related to it, but it has a defensive purpose to keep itself in power and so maintain the status quo. The main aim seems to be to prevent the weakening of the organisation and to control the members of the gang so that they will not desert the destructive organisation and join the positive parts of the self or betray the secrets of the gang to the Police, the protecting super-ego, standing for the helpful analyst, who might be able to save the patient. Frequently, when a patient of this kind makes progress in analysis and wants to change, he dreams of being attacked by members of the Mafia or adolescent delinquents, and a negative therapeutic reaction sets in. [Rosenfeld, 1987, pp. 111–112]

This is very relevant for the internal world of people with a terrorist history. In Northern Ireland the mind of internal Loyalist (UVF, UDA, UFF, Red Hand Commandos) or Republican (IRA, Real IRA, Continuity IRA, INLA) and state security and political force exert enormous internal control of destructive impulses. As we have seen from the words of Collins and Stone, there are massive internal propaganda machines that justify the idealization of the death instinct. Furthermore, initial movements to a more creative and "life instinct" style of human relations are met with internal accusations of weakness and humiliation. It is only when the rewards of a more positive style of relating are truly experienced that the individual is able to feel that hatred can be given up. This is where good experiences have to abound, so that all hard men, paramilitary, academic, professional, and middle-class terrorists alike, have an experience of human coupling that brings warmth and intimacy rather than hostility and paranoia. But as Rosenfeld (1987) argues, good experiences will often be rejected or spoiled, usually by envy, in the service of maintaining the status quo. It is important, therefore, that all of us should be resilient with good experiences, and prevent them being perverted into bad experiences with the hope that creative experiences will win through.

The formation of a new depressive position identity, it could be argued, is beginning to happen. Current attempts to deal with, and resolve, conflict, however difficult, has provided a window where people can experiment with a more human and softer style of relating. For example, it may be argued that the society is experiencing a type of post-Oedipal thirdness allowing for a more mature relationship with its near neighbours, the Republic of Ireland and Britain, and those further afield in the USA and Europe. We are also considering the concerns of the international "other", hearing and listening to those who have been persecuted elswhere in the world.

There is great potential for the development of more reparative relationships between ourselves and others as we gradually leave violence behind and progress towards a more equal and mutually dependent society. For this identity (or perhaps more accurately, these identities) to retain strength and value, the real benefits of generous and giving human relationships have to be recognized, so that the idealization of hate is dissipated. This involves a constant working and re-working of positive and fulfilling human relations so that internalization of good experiences/objects can take place in everyday life.

Sadism

Sadism is an excited state of mind which gives pleasure, however short-term, as a substitute for pleasure and satisfaction through kindness and human warmth (Kapur, 2004). Cruelty becomes the main mode of relating, fuelled by endless envy of others. It is when this becomes the predominant mode of relating that states of terror become the hallmark of day-to-day relationships. In a society exposed to so much destructiveness it is not surprising that pleasure has become attached to so much negative behaviour.

Relinquishing pleasure attached to cruelty is also a complex process. The creation of social conditions that provide opportunities for good experiences to take place, and that have kindness and generosity attached to them, is crucial. As we have highlighted many times in this book, there is always difficulty in offering goodness when paranoid anxieties are rampant. Conversely, to create a less troubled mind there have to be places and events that are delivered out of a wish and intention to make things better. This can be achieved at different social levels, interpersonal, familial, organizational, and institutional. When these positive and practical events take place, people have a chance to attach their pleasure to positive events and gain satisfaction and excitement from these. Society and the political structures have to make a real effort to offer a "bountiful breast", which, if the recipients' state of mind is less troubled, can be taken with pleasure rather than attacked, or bitten, or, more seriously, perverted into a negative experience.

It may be that the peace process in Northern Ireland can create a space where generosity and goodwill can flourish over the attachment of excitement and pleasure to cruelty. Culturally we see more events occurring in this society, with events and activities from other parts of the world providing a glimpse of pluralism and demonstrating how difference and diversity can be enjoyed rather than treated with suspicion. It may be that the government has been slow to offer positive experiences which improve the well being of individuals, but initiatives such as the creation of the Equality Commission and the Human Rights Commission is a positive signal to people that there is a wish to create a more equal society where every citizen's humanity is valued and attempts are made to protect it. If people feel secure in the knowledge that "big brother" is looking after them in a positive way, then there is less chance of people gaining satisfaction from inflicting cruelty on others. Here, the mechanism of reparative guilt is important in that if the individual realizes that they are indeed spoiling good experiences to obtain a perverse pleasure, then there is a real possibility that people can take from the hand that feeds them, rather than attack it.

Paranoia

"Whatever you say, say nothing" is a phrase coined by Seamus Heaney and used by some commentators to describe an aspect of the troubled mind we have talked about in this book. Klein's concept of paranoid–schizoid functioning helps us to explain and understand the suspicion and distrust that permeates a personality exposed to destructive processes. This is an inevitable part of a society characterized by the death instinct. So how do relationships change? Within therapeutic processes the only way out of paranoid–schizoid functioning is the opening up of trust and intimacy in human relationships. This, of course, involves vulnerability to attack, and a "hard man" personality will have developed a tough skin over many years of trauma, loss, and disappointment. This concept of a psychic skin or membrane to hold together states of mind has been referred to by Kleinian writers such as Mitrani (2001) following the work of Riech (1949) and others such as Tustin. Here, we can use this concept of "psychic skin" to refer to the hard skin that is associated with the withdrawn and paranoid relatedness that inevitably comes from a traumatized state of mind.

In taking forward clinical work with traumatized patients, the hallmark of all psychodynamic and psychoanalytic approaches is the achievement of creating a feeling of safety, what Wilson (1989) refers to as the therapeutic membrane where traumas and anxieties can be explored. In highlighting the importance of social support for survivors of war, Herman writes of the trauma experienced by soldiers.

> Once a sense of safety has been re-established, the survivor needs the help of others in re-building a positive view of the self. The regulation of intimacy and aggression, disrupted by the trauma, must be restored. This requires that others show some tolerance for the survivor's fluctuating need for closeness and distance, and some respect for her attempts to re-establish autonomy and self control . . . Many returning soldiers speak of their difficulties with intimacy and aggression. The combat veteran, Michael Norman, testifies to these difficulties, "unsettled and irritable, I behaved badly, I sought solitude, then slandered friends for keeping away . . . I barked at a son who revered me and bickered at my best ally, my wife. [Herman, 1992, p. 63]

Feeling safe and creating experiences of safety are crucial in re-establishing the normality of ordinary intimacy and human warmth in day-to-day relatedness in Northern Ireland. Here, the onus is very much on people to take responsibility for how they relate to others. The "blame game" fits so neatly into the victim's game in preventing self-reflection and subsequent personal responsibility for negative comments and actions. For a paranoid state of mind to be dissolved there is a huge requirement on all of us to provide more good experiences over bad. Clinically, within the consulting room, psychoanalysts and psychotherapists are very familiar with this basic need to establish trust and safety. Technically, it can only be done by hard work in the here and now of the professional relationship, where trust is slowly re-established after the patient or client receives positive experiences of being helped and understood. Similarly, this is the only way it can happen with the troubled mind of Northern Ireland. There is no short-cut to trust. It may be that after this process is allowed to take place everyday conversations will be characterized by "whatever you say, say something" followed by "'The something' I say will be good rather than bad."

Dependence

Depending on others in a mutually beneficial and reciprocal way is a necessary pre-condition for the fulfilment of ordinary human relationships where emotional and physical needs can be met. In a society troubled by conflict it tends to be the case that relying on others is too dangerous (a phenomenon described in earlier chapters), relationships become characterized by death and destruction, and no one can be trusted. However, for society to work, particularly within the depressive position, concern for others based on a real and positive experience of dependence is essential.

This achievement of mutual dependence on others is particularly difficult within a society characterized by the hard man mentality, where self-sufficiency is overvalued and needs are met through more violent and perverse human relationships. Again, this clinical phenomena is well known in the consulting room, where there is often an intense opposition from the patient to relying on anyone else for help. This is a central part of the manic defences described in Chapter Two and illustrated by many examples in subsequent chapters. A central feature of the troubled mind of Northern Ireland is the intense polarization of good and bad into the two religious groups, which justifies a self-sufficient and non-dependent response between the two communities. However, the synergy of both coming together in a mutually dependent and enriching way is inevitably lost when there is such a drive for independence in thoughts and behaviour.

There are, however, different forms of dependence, some purposeful, others damaging, and it could be argued that Northern Irish society has tended to have an infantile dependence with other countries. For example, during long periods of direct rule, and more recently when the local assembly was suspended, there was an expectation on the part of some sections of politics and society that the British or Irish governments should somehow rescue the situation. The experience of not being able to handle our own affairs has had a disabling affect on the capacity for change. In infantile, dependent relationships, all the strengths and, thus, individual confidence of the lesser partner leaks away. It is only when the dominant partner, either in the wider political setting or the intimacy of everyday relationships, gives back the strengths and talents to the other person, that equality and mutual interdependence can flower. Farren and Mulvihill illustrate the anxieties of the Unionist communities when the dependent relationship with the British Government was threatened by the Anglo-Irish Agreement.

> The Anglo-Irish Agreement had several very important effects on the Unionist–Loyalist elements of the population, most notably with respect to the historic settler–covenantal relationship to which we assigned so much importance. First, Unionist dependency on, and collusive behaviour with, Britain was diminished greatly ... the history of Unionism is replete with settler and covenantal themes of dependence derived from the inability of the Protestant settlers to provide for their own security. Unionists frequently called on Lord Randolph Churchill's famous "Orange Card" in order to avoid abandonment. Since the imposition of Direct Rule that dependency had deepened. Northern Ireland was, by the mid-1980s, without a locally elected Government of its own for nearly a quarter of its existence. Richard Sennet warns that dependency almost always results in a paradoxical form of negation (recreated in the fear of extinction) where the dependent party maintains the appearance of independence by criticising the authoritative actor. Dependence is thereby disguised. (Farren & Mulvihill, 2000, p. 137]

We have to re-own that which we have projected on to others and develop new forms of relatedness built on confidence and mutual dependence with those who have been our enemies.

Envy

Throughout the book we have consistently referred to envy as one of the most destructive emotions in the troubled mind of Northern Ireland. It is a silent killer. Envy is often the hidden deeper motive behind destructive attacks on others. Whether it is the envy of other people's talents or simply their good fortune or emotional intelligence, envy kills human creativity and development. Betty Joseph, who sought to apply Klein's original concept of envy to everyday life, succinctly writes:

> What I want to do now is look at envy as we see it operating in everyday life and then consider some of its implications. The conscious end we all know about, in a sense—feelings of resentment at someone being ahead, doing better, and vague hostility, rivalry, competitiveness—but it is when it is more powerful that the trouble starts; for example, when it leads to a kind of constant carping criticism or snide remarks or the other way around, when the envious individual cannot see anything to praise or value in another individual, but always finds doubts, "well it was good but . . ." and he will find some reason to doubt or knock the other person. And as there really always is some ground for criticism in any of us in what we do, the envious attitude can easily be missed and the criticism or doubts can look real.

And she goes onto highlight the destructiveness of spoiling attacks.

> The manifestations of envy that concern us more here are those more clearly associated with spoiling—spoiling being fundamental to envy. The envious person can spoil literally by mud-slinging, damaging, or hurting another person or his possession; or he can spoil by psychological mud-slinging, hurting, another person's attributes or achievements in his own mind, in his thinking or externally by criticism, mockery, or provocation. I say "provocation" because it is a marvellous spoiler, well known to many people, often very visible say in adolescence and in psychoanalytic treatment. We can see this kind of thing when the envious person

envies the other person's quiet intelligence and peace of mind and
sets about to needle and provoke until the other loses his cool. This
can be a very clear weapon in analysis. [Joseph, 1989, p.183]

We can identify such phenomena in the everyday life of
Northern Ireland. Academics sometimes make spoiling attacks on
non-academics as they cannot bear their non-academic talents,
whether those lie in the hands of a carpenter or in the skill, artistry,
and femininity of a hairdresser. Middle-class professionals will
attack working-class people, perhaps secretly envious of the sense
of collectivity and togetherness that characterizes such communities. Of course, this can be a two-way process, with disadvantaged
people being resentful of those middle-class, well-educated sections
of society, but at least here the envy appears more visible. It is often
the envious and spoiling attacks of the so-called better off that
can suffocate human creativity and development. In the troubled
mind of Northern Ireland, it is sometimes the case that those in
authority warmly and creatively identify the talents of others so
that they flourish. This can occur across all walks of life: universities, schools, or the workplace. The annihilation of the other
person's confidence is seen as the only way to get even. The talents
and abilities of the other person are unbearable and the only way
to deal with this feeling of not having what the other person has is
to enviously attack them.

In our analysis, these envious attacks have a particular quality
of a troubled mind that has suffered terrorism. Envious people
launch "terrorist" attacks in the way they have witnessed and experienced for over thirty-five years. People with talent and ability are
ambushed and "sniped at" without warning. Often a well planned
and orchestrated attack is made on individuals showing flair and
talent, where all the stupidity and inadequacy of the attacker is
projected into the "target". These types of experiences have been
reported elsewhere (Rice & Kapur, 2002). The legitimization of
these attacks is to "put people in their place". As noted in Brenman
(1995) the justification for cruelty is a moralization of destructiveness in the belief that it is bringing justice and doing good.

Taking from others who have talents and abilities we do not
have, with gratitude, is one way out of this destructiveness. A
precursor to this is to recognize that we all have strengths and

weaknesses, in doing so giving up our phantasies and beliefs of omnipotence. By coupling with the strengths of others to deal with our own weaknesses, we can all live happier and fulfilling lives. Being grateful and enjoying the talents of others rather than wishing to kill off vitality and hope, allows for growth and creativity. This has to be the new language of a more peaceful Northern Ireland. Joseph points to these benefits of a non-envious state of mind.

> Perhaps all I can say at this stage is that ordinarily we could hope that the individual has sufficient available affection and love, and capacity to feel warmth and gratitude, to be able to counter-balance his rivalry and his envy, and yet be aware of its existence and allow other human beings to be seen as worthy of envy. [Joseph, 1986, pp. 190–191]

Recognizing and allowing the talents of others to grow while holding back envious feelings contained by a recognition of your own talents can stop the awful destructiveness and angst that goes with nasty envious attacks that, like a good terrorist, disappear without trace and are never identified. It is up to our consciences to prevent us launching such attacks, and if they do occur, make an honest reparation. It is this reparation that we consider in the conclusion of this psychoanalytic analysis.

Reparation

> The pain of mourning experienced in the depressive position and the reparative drives developed to restore the loved internal and external objects, are the basis of creativity and sublimation. These reparative activities are directed towards both the object and the self. They are done partly because of concern for and guilt towards the object, and the wish to restore, preserve and give it eternal life; and partly in the interest of self-preservation, now more realistically orientated. The infant's longing to recreate his lost objects gives him the impulse to put together what has been torn assunder, to reconstruct what has been destroyed, to recreate and to create. At the same time, his wish to spare his objects leads him to sublimate his impulses when they are felt to be destructive. [Segal, 1973, p. 75]

Making good harm done to others is the essential ingredient of any reconciliation process. However, in most models of conflict resolution and truth seeking, the individual's capacity for human destructiveness is rarely given centre stage. Sometimes institutional attempts at seeking reparation are flawed because those who reveal their trauma are not supported and do not gain any therapeutic benefits from the process, as has been noted earlier in this book in reference to the South African Truth and Reconciliation Commission (Kaminer *et al.*, 2001). Much is also written and talked about in Northern Ireland about the need for forgiveness; we believe that mechanisms must be found to reduce the capacity of people to harm others with acts of verbal and physical destruction and to activate reparative guilt in an everyday, here and now, way. In doing so it may be possible to contain and detoxify the impulse of destructiveness that has been part of the troubled mind of Northern Ireland.

This reparative urge is activated when there is a feeling that harm has been done to others. In discussing this crucial psychological change, which leads to creative relationships, Segal quotes from work with a child who began to own and "name" her aggressive impulses.

> In that way, she gave me an opportunity to interpret directly in the transference her repeated attacks on me, and the task of reparation she was faced with if she wanted me to continue being a good analyst to her. [Segal, 1973, p. 100]

By drawing attention to the negative attacks on her, Segal was bringing to the child's awareness the unconscious destructiveness which, up to this time, she had not been conscious of. Segal adds:

> With this change went also a changed attitude to myself; she accepted me as a whole person, father, who made reparation to herself and to her mother, and helped her to do such reparation as she could. There was an acknowledgement of need and dependence on both parents, and of the necessity to have them both restored and to have their help in the process of reparation. At the same time, there was an acknowledgement not only of aggression in the past, but of continuing aggression. [Segal, 1973, p. 101]

It is this continuing aggression, often fuelled out of envy and a hatred of dependence, that is a hallmark of a troubled mind. Until there is a societal guilt about what we can do to each other, then the troubled mind will continue. Here, it is important to differentiate between genuine reparation involving guilt and concern at what has been done to others and manic reparation, which avoids the pain of guilt and puts an emotional plaster over emotional destructiveness. Segal succinctly describes this.

Manic reparation is a defence in that its aim is to repair the object in such a way that guilt and loss are never experienced. An essential feature of manic reparation is that it has to be done without acknowledgement of guilt, and therefore under special conditions. For instance, manic reparation is never done in relation to primary objects or internal objects, but always in relation to remote objects; secondly, the object in relation to which reparation is done must never be experienced as having been damaged by oneself; thirdly, the object must be felt as inferior, dependent and, at depth, contemptible. There can be no time, love or esteem for the object or objects that are being repaired, as this would threaten the return of true depressive feelings. [Segal, 1973, pp. 95–96]

In the current peace process we may be guilty of manic reparation. Political and social changes have occurred, together with a significant lessening of paramilitary activity. A new police force has been formed, Equality and Human Rights Commissions established. These are important structural changes, which have had a positive effect by creating the possibility that society can function in a peaceful, civilized, and equal way that protects the human rights of individuals. However, a deeper change has to take place to ensure this is not simply manic reparation, which deals only with surface phenomena. For real reparation to take place, there has to be a humanization in the peace process that replaces the demonization of human beings. This is where, as stated many times in this book, individuals have to take responsibility for their behaviour towards others. People affect people. So it follows that if everyone takes more responsibility for how they relate to each other then "ripple" and "top-down, bottom-up" effects can take place, so creating a culture of concern to replace a culture of hate and projection. As in other wars and conflicts we have to "own what we've done"—in other words, to activate the reparative impulse. This is not about triggering a guilt-trip; rather it is about launching a movement towards more humane day-to-day relations. Cohen refers to the "guilt-tripping" that prevents real reparation.

> Appeals like "skip lunch, save a child" look simple, pragmatic and unemotional. But the not-so-hidden subtext is that if you don't comply with this undemanding request, you will feel guilty. How else can you live, knowing that this token amount of money lets you arbitrate between life and death. [Cohen, p. 182]

Prior to the ceasefires here, the government ran such campaigns appealing to the public to pass information on the "Confidential Telephone Line" to the security forces to help prevent killings. It could be argued that the government was trying to invoke guilt yet denied their own guilt in creating an unjust society that could only breed terrorism and hate. In this respect, security forces have to accept guilt and responsibility for their part in state terrorism; there is little point in creating campaigns to make other groups feel guilty when there is an abject failure to take responsibility for the actions of the state. There are no situations where terror wholly belongs only to one side. It is only when there is a collective approach to engagement in a reparative process at personal, cultural, and institutional levels that humanization, equality, and justice can occur.

Creating the conditions for reparation

In the first chapter we drew attention to the social, political, and economic context of Northern Irish society. We believe that there are a number of practical interventions that can be made to create the conditions for a more reparative society. For example, the core of many of our divisions is an educational system that splits individuals into good and bad in a number of ways. The continued existence of the 11+ assessment method and the grammar school system sustains this splitting, leading to feelings of social superiority by those "well educated" and those "not well educated". This system cuts across sectarian and, sometimes, class divides. Thus, Catholics and Protestants, as well as working-class children who make the "golden cut" and enter the grammar school system, aged eleven, often become socialized into believing that they must be superior to those who have not. Such a profound event, which allocates most of society's intelligence to particular minority groups by virtue of a test that many educational psychologists agree is faulty, creates a division that provides a ready-made receptacle for the good and bad parts of society.

Any real change in Northern Ireland has to facilitate an integration of these splits. To some extent this has occurred with the relative success and growth of the integrated education movement, although this has still to reach more than 10% of the population. However, even this positive change has fallen under the influence of the grammar system as grammar and non-grammar streams are being set up within these integrated schools. It is important for this society to resist the global allocation of intelligence to one group or other and to seek other measures of achievement. The concept of emotional intelligence (Coleman, 1995) places value on the quality of human relations, in a similar way to the depressive state in Kleinian theory, rather than a schizoid relation that many people have to the value of IQ. So what would this look like? How could this society, so riddled by this intelligence split, value different aspects of daily life rather than placing their good feelings into an artificial categorization that only perpetuates paranoid–schizoid functioning?

First, the attitudes to learning have to change. The university of life has to be valued as much as the university of books. Wisdom and maturity, as represented in the depressive position functioning of concern, retrieving projections, taking value and pride in the achievements of others, has to become part and parcel of a new state of mind that welcomes talent of all sorts. This psychological pluralism immunizes society from the cruelty of depriving good people of value and worthiness in carrying out good deeds. The preoccupation with letters after names and meaningless titles only serves to perpetuate a troubled mind. University rituals are particularly guilty of conferring titles that offer a desperate external validation of deep-down inadequacy that has been projected on to those who did not pass their 11+ and/or go to university. For this to change, it has to come from the top. Leaders are given the responsibility to lead with maturity and concern and those with "academic intelligence" cannot continue to project their own inadequacies elsewhere.

Second, an ownership of personal inadequacies and limitations dissolves the psychotic omnipotence associated with paranoid–schizoid relationships. The idea of brains over beauty creates a vehicle for a nasty spoiling attack on the vulnerabilities through an evacuation of unbearable inadequacies into non-academics. It is human to err and part of the humanization process that is needed is to seek to limit the bad parts of ourselves we place in others. This is certainly true around the allocation of labels of stupidity and intelligence in Northern Irish society. Perhaps a different categorization should be used as follows:

- *Stupidity* To be stupid is to be cruel and, in a flash, evacuate bad feelings and thoughts about yourself into others. Stupidity is also characterized by a possessiveness of titles, letters, and status which serve only to cleanse an inadequate and flawed personality of his or her own failures and fundamental badness and cruelty. Stupidity is over-valuing a faulty 11+-based grammar school system and an academically limited local university system that is fundamentally flawed in this artificial allocation of intelligence according to its paranoid–schizoid system of thinking and relating.

- *Intelligence* To be intelligent is to be wise and mature in human relations and value all talents from brains to beauty. Motherhood, femininity, and aesthetic qualities are given equivalence to PhDs and academic degrees. Intelligence is associated with a distinct concern for your impact on others where the whole person is taken into account while taking personal responsibility for the impact of yourself on others. Good is the territory of all talents rather than a chosen few pre-selected by an archaic method of categorizing superiority and inferiority.

Finally, this attitudinal change among the elite of Northern Ireland has to permeate into public policy. The legacy of a paranoid–schizoid definition of intelligence has left a lineage of policy-makers who put resources into perpetuating a troubled mind with distorted values and principles. The education system is a good starting point for less split thinking. The current review of the 11+-based grammar school system in Northern Ireland has offered an alternative, more "intelligent" way of allocating resources and giving everyone a chance to fulfil their potential across the vocational/academic spectrum. Inevitably, there is opposition to this radical change, but those resisting the humanization of what we define as intelligence are only perpetuating troubled human relations that will eventually continue the unhappiness and suffering associated with such a narrow paranoid–schizoid definition. This wish to retain the status quo values a schizoid/withdrawn style of human relatedness that continues insularity rather than allowing pluralism and a fuller engagement in day-to-day life.

A similar critique can be applied to other social divisions in this society. A recurrent theme in the analysis of the emotional effects of the troubles, using this Kleinian theoretical framework, is the pervasive nature of splitting in everyday life. This is apparent, inevitably, in the distribution of wealth and the existence of clear working- and social class categories. Bizarrely, as stated above in relation to education, this permeates the sectarian divide and in many instances acts as an integration of the two different religious groups; for example middle-class Protestants and Catholics often mix socially while ignoring "their own" working-class religious groups. This strict adherence to boundaries of class, with the associated distribution of greater wealth for the middle or professional classes, provides yet another, if it were needed, opportunity for negative feelings and thoughts to be disowned and projected into others.

As stated earlier, this is most noticeable where all styles of terrorist relating are allocated to the working classes, where paramilitaries have their main strength and support. Yet, as also previously highlighted, much terrorist activity occurs through middle-class wars either in the courtroom or the workplace. The middle class often disown their use of fear and intimidation, yet act out these very behaviours in their day-to-day human relations. Greed, a characteristic of paranoid–schizoid functioning, which temporarily fills people up through material gain in order to deal with emotional poverty, is valued as a way of justifying what may be the pursuit of wealth for the purpose of greed, rather than earning a livelihood. The irony is that these forms of greed are often rationalized as positive whereas more explicit forms of violence that occur in working-class areas is so often vilified. An "unthinkable thought" is the realization that the use of fear and intimidation is as rife in middle-class human relations as it is in those of the working class, with the former finding less visible ways of acting out their similar "paranoid–schizoid" state of mind. The style of terrorist relatedness is the same, the content different. So what must happen for things to change?

Fundamentally, the middle classes, sheltered by their wealth and fortune, have to retrieve their terrorist projections from the working classes. This implies more than a redistribution of wealth; it means a redistribution of where the troubled human relations are really located. The success of the middle classes in splitting off from the troubles of the last thirty-five years has led to a disowning of a style of human relations that is no worse, albeit not as concrete, as their working-class counterparts.

It is the professional and middle classes, of course, who benefit from the establishment system in Northern Ireland, which not only guarantees "jobs for the boys" but reinforces middle-class lineage, so depriving working classes, irrespective of their religion, of a fair chance of better opportunities. Of course, the provision of greater opportunities for the empowerment of working class communities is essential, through, for example, government initiatives such as "Targeting Social Need". But those who have need to model better human relationships, both with themselves and with those who have not. This important role modelling and facilitation would not only allow a diffusion of economic splits but would also maximize depressive position functioning.

In turning to politics, we can see that the landscape is changing in Northern Ireland. For fifty years, until the early part of the Troubles in the late 1960s, it can be argued that the Unionist bloc abused power and manipulated a flawed democratic system that did not offer fellow citizens, usually Catholics, full political and social citizenship. Farren and Mulvihill describe this history as follows:

Northern Ireland was, therefore, from its inception, deeply divided in virtually every aspect of communal life, its deep patterns of segregation most readily identifiable in terms of religious affiliation. In housing, education and employment, perhaps the three most important markers of inter-community division, separation was such as to ensure that for long social contact across any of these boundaries was minimal. Each community was endogamous, while the region's political institutions, rather than providing meeting places in which conflict could be resolved, merely reinforced division at every level. From 1921 until the Northern Ireland parliament was abolished in 1972, the Unionist Party usually held forty of the fifty-two seats in its House of Commons, the Nationalist (Catholic) Party the remainder. Excluded from any meaningful role in either Government or administration, the latter played only a desultory role in parliament, attending with little regularity and participating most vigorously only when issues affecting its own community were under discussion, such as education, housing and the partition of Ireland. [Farren & Mulvihill, 2000, p. 17]

Now the picture is somewhat different. Smaller political groups, representing all spectrums of society from Republican (Sinn Fein) to Loyalist paramilitaries (Progressive Unionist Party) and women (Women's Coalition) now have a stronger political base that seems to encourage a greater sense of pluralism in this once barren political landscape. By the very nature of this political growth, the negative aspects of splitting have been diffused, with people experiencing the fact that shades of different political opinion can exist. There are several other important emotional and psychological aspects of this change.

First, and most important, different leadership styles have emerged that rely less on idealization and an unquestioning dependence on the leader (basic assumption functioning). The leadership of such politicians as David Ervine (Progressive Unionist Party) and Monica McWilliams (Women's Coalition) relies less on authoritarian directions and compliance with strict rules and instructions and more on "thinking" about political issues with debate and discussion rather than the aggressive bullying "tactics" so common in Northern Irish political discourses. In Sinnerton (2002), Ervine refers to this when recounting his experience in what he calls "Spence University" (prison).

Disillusion translated into Spence's re-evaluating his Unionism and himself. He found it to be a difficult personal experience. If you are truthful, self-questioning is the most hurtful aspect of human nature—to admit responsibility. [Sinnerton, 2002, p. 80]

He adds:

Although decidedly left-wing and unorthodox, Spence pitched his policy securely within the Unionist fold. He laid out his principle for Unionism without compromise or ambiguity. Anyone who is for the Union could be a Unionist. He stated that a Unionism that is genuine and reasonable should be honestly and openly argued. [Sinnerton, 2002, p. 88]

The important aspect of this new style of leadership is the emphasis on "thinking" rather than acting, an essential characteristic of depressive position functioning. This allows debate to flourish and, in thinking through processes, issues can be resolved in a sane and wise way, rather than relying on forced solutions that only result in compliance and flawed solutions. It is this type of leadership that can promote more "work group" functioning, so ensuring time and full engagement of all players in Northern Ireland society.

Second, a related and important potential within such changing political scenery is the hope for an inclusive approach in which all views, green, orange, and those in between, can be expressed. This political pluralism allows for an enrichment of views and, by the very nature of politicians meeting and talking with each other, prevents prejudice and stereotyping taking over. Extreme views, as judged by the old politics of the 1960s, are now acceptable and part and parcel of vibrant political life. With the different shades of green and orange being represented, the possibility exists of finer judgements and debates occurring, rather than an immediate argument with anyone of a different view, leading to a regression to warfare between "us and them". Now, "bits of us" and "bits of them" are merging across the full political spectrum. Politicians are now being forced to think of the minutiae of policies affecting their community rather than thinking that it is simply a Unionist or Nationalist issue. It could be an extreme Unionist or Nationalist issue versus a more modern Unionist or Progressive issue.

While these shades are flourishing, the voices of black, brown, and other ethnic minority communities is still unclear. While some of the Chinese, Asian, and Black communities have loose affiliations to some of the political groups, they do not yet feel safe to have a separate and unique political voice. Feelings of "it's not really our country" and "who are we to have a say" still permeate ethnic minority thinking. Ethnic minorities are still unsure as to how warm the welcome will be into influencing public life. My own experience (RK) is mixed. As the first brown face running a white public sector organization and the first brown face making a regular contribution to local radio (BBC Radio Ulster/Talkback), I have felt two things. First, when taking up these jobs, an uncertainty about whether the voice of Indians deserved to be heard and were important enough in a society dominated by green and orange issues. Had I a right to express my views?

I have certainly felt in these and other similar roles that I have jumped the queue ahead of female Catholics and WASPs (white Anglo-Saxon Protestants), who feel they should be at the front of the queue again after giving so much ground, in their eyes, to Catholics. Then I felt, why not! We're all from the same human race and my brain cells function just as well as anyone else's. My position to make a contribution is all the stronger because I am Northern Irish born and bred. It will be difficult for those not born here to feel their contribution is both valued and valid. Perhaps it is only when ethnic minorities are able to fulfil political roles that we can truly feel we have political pluralism in the depressive position.

Finally, an important change that has occurred and will require consolidation and development, is the move from the bullet to the ballot box. This succinctly describes the movement from paranoid–schizoid to depressive position functions where words and thoughts replace bullets and action. In Kleinian terminology, this also represents a subtle movement from concrete functioning in the paranoid–schizoid position, where little meaning is attached to acts, to the development of the capacity for symbol formation (Segal, 1985), where meaning, imagery and other forms of creative expression can be used to communicate internal worlds. For whatever reason, whether it is an internal or external process, a large majority have been able to turn away from violence to using politics as a way of furthering their views.

This movement has meant that dialogue and communication between different groups has become more possible. Political groups linked to paramilitary organizations, such as the Progressive Unionist Party and Sinn Fein, have regular contact with each other and welcome debate and discussion. This has even led to each side publicly acknowledging the views and positions of the other and the anxieties of either being forced into a political agreement they may dislike. Force has been replaced with the freedom to debate, consider each other's view and shift position as and when issues have been thoroughly discussed. This movement has also recently permeated to local community conflicts where politicians from both sides realize the wastefulness of local violence in wrecking their own communities and express concern at the effect of each other's action on the other. The re-channelling of political ambitions into democratic processes is a vital part of Northern Ireland lessening its troubled mind and embracing a more civilized approach to power and politics.

However, not all political parties have embraced this willingness for dialogue. Parties such as the Democratic Unionist Party and the United Kingdom Unionist Party see such contact, particularly with political groups such as Sinn Fein, who are linked to the Provisional IRA, as desecrating the graves of people they have known in the security forces who have been murdered. These parties see such contact and dialogue as a sign of weakness, and mistrust the move to politics as part of a terrorist plot to force them into a political agreement they dislike via the back door. Some Ulster Unionist politicians within the anti-agreement camp also hold this view, and remain entrenched. Final recognition of the democratic process would be the IRA publicly giving up their weapons. For the IRA and Republicans this would be seen as an act of humiliation perpetrated by a Unionist community who have never really given up their triumphalism. So what is the truth?

Clearly the concepts of paranoid–schizoid and depressive position function can be used interchangeably to support particular views. However, the central aspects of paranoid–schizoid functioning relates to whether destructiveness is perpetuated. In our view, no linkage or communication between any individual group can only reinforce schizoid relatedness and so confirm or increase paranoia. Acceptance of the sincerity of paramilitary moves to democratic politics involves the "hard man" aspect of suspicious politicians "trusting in the process". But there is no other way to move to depressive position functioning and a less troubled mind. If trust is misplaced, then the loss of trust has to be mourned and a security found in a regression to a more paranoid style of relatedness. However, if the move from the bullet to the ballot box is not embraced, then destructive violence has more chance to flourish.

One final point we wish to make in this book, is that any political changes that have taken place, and have to continue to take place for more depressive position functioning, will have an impact on day-to-day human relations in Northern Ireland. As we have stated repeatedly, a top-down and bottom-up approach to human relations has to take place for real change to happen. It is only when everyone, politicians and people on the street, take responsibility for the way in which they relate to others that peace and calm can return to everyday life. We hope this book gives you food for thought as to how you can think differently about how you relate to troubled states of mind, whether here or in other contexts, and help in a more human approach to how we relate to each other today. Perhaps the lessons learned from the troubled mind of Northern Ireland can be a source of learning and experience elsewhere in a world that is now troubled by global terrorism. Addressing the effects of our internal terrorist on ourselves and others, rather than projecting into defined terrorist groups, might make a small but significant difference to the lives we lead.

REFERENCES

Anderson, R. (1992). *Clinical Lectures on Klein and Bion*. London: Routledge.

Bahia, A. B. (1981). New theories: their influence and effect on psychoanalytic technique. In: J. S. Grotstein (Ed.), *Do I Dare Disturb the Universe: A Memorial to W. R. Bion* (pp. 239–268). London: Karnac.

Bardon, J. (2001). *A History of Ulster*. Belfast: Blackstaff.

Benson, J. (1992). The group turned inwards: a consideration of some group phenomena as reflective of the Northern Irish situation. *Groupwork, 5*(3): 5–18.

Benson, J. (1994). The secret war in the dis-United Kingdom: psychological aspects of the Ulster conflict. *Group Analysis, 28*: 47–62.

Bion, W. R. (1957). Differentiation of the psychotic from the non-psychotic personalities. In: *Second Thoughts*. London: Karnac, 1993, (pp. 43–64).

Bion, W. R. (1958). On arrogance. *International Journal of Psychoanalysis, 39*: 144–146 [reprinted in *Second Thoughts*, London: Karnac, 1993, pp. 86–92].

Bion, W. R. (1959a). Attacks on linking. *International Journal of Psychoanalysis, 40*: 308–305 [reprinted in *Second Thoughts*, London: Karnac, 1993, pp. 943–109].

Bion, W. R. (1959b). *Experiences in Groups*. New York. Basic Books.

Bion, W. R. (1962). *Learning from Experience*. London: Heinemann (1984).

Birrell, D., & Murie, A. (1980). *Policy and Government in Northern Ireland: Lessons from Devolution*. Dublin: Gill and Macmillan.

Bloomer, F., & Weinreich, P. (2003). Cross community relations projects and inter-dependent identities. In: O. Hargie & D. Dickson (Eds.), *Researching the Troubles: Social Science Perspectives and the Northern Ireland Conflict* (pp. 141–162). Edinburgh & London: Mainstream.

Bloomfield, K. (1998). *We Will Remember Them: Report of the Northern Ireland Victims' Commissions*. Belfast: HMSO.

Borooah, V. K. (1993). A typology of a regional economy. In: P. Teague (Ed.), *The Economy of Northern Ireland: Perspectives for Structural Change* (pp. 1–23). London: Lawrence & Wishart.

Brenman, E. (1995). Cruelty and narrow mindedness. *International Journal of Psychoanalysis, 66,* 273–281 [reprinted in E. B. Spillius, (Ed.) *Melanie Klein Today, Vol. 1: Mainly Theory* London: Routledge, pp. 256–271].

Brewer, J. D. (1991). The parallels between sectarianism and racism: the Northern Ireland experience. In: CCETSW (Ed.), *Improving Social Work Education and Training Paper No. 8* (pp. 85–108). London: CCETSW.

Britton, R. (1992) The Oedipus situation and the depressive position,. In: R. Anderson (Ed.), *Clinical Lectures on Klein and Bion* (pp. 34–45). London: Routledge.

Britton, R., Feldman, M., & O'Shaughnessy, E. (1989). *The Oedipus Complex Today: Clinical Implications*. London: Karnac.

Brunet, L., & Casoni, D. (1991). Terrorism: attack on internal objects. *Melanie Klein and Object Relations, 9*(1): 1–15.

Cairns, E., & Wilson, R. (1989). Mental health aspects of political violence in Northern Ireland. *International Journal of Mental Health, 18*(1): 38–56.

Campbell, J., & Healey, A. (1999). "Whatever you say, say something": the education, training and practice of mental health social workers in Northern Ireland. *Social Work Education, 18*(4): 389–400.

Campbell, J., & McLaughlin, J. (2002). The "joined-up" management of adult health and social care servies in Northern Ireland: Lessons for the rest of the UK. *Managing Community Care, 8*(5): 6–12.

Campbell, J., & Pinkerton, J. (1997). Embracing change as opportunity: reflections on social work from a Northern Ireland perspective. In: B. Lesnik (Ed.), *Change in Social Work* (pp. 45–66). Aldershot: Arena.

Cohen, S. (2001). *States of Denial: Knowing About Atrocities and Suffering*. Cambridge: Blackwell.

Coleman, D. (1995). *Emotional Intelligence*. London: Bloomsbury.

Collins, E. (1997). *Killing Rage*. London. Grants Books.

Connolly, P., & Healy, J. (2003). The development of children's attitudes towards the "Troubles" in Northern Ireland. In: O. Hargie & D. Dickson (Eds.), *Researching the Troubles: Social Science Perspectives and the Northern Ireland Conflict* (pp. 37–58). Edinburgh & London: Mainstream.

Coulter, C. (1999). *Contemporary Northern Irish Society: An introduction*. London: Pluto.

Cullberg-Weston, M. (1997). When words lose their meaning: from societal crisis to ethnic cleansing. *Mind and Human Interaction, 8*: 20–32.

Darby, J., & MacGinty, R. (2003). Coming out of violence. A comparative study of the peace processes. In: O. Hargie & D. Dickson (Eds.), *Researching the Troubles: Social Science Perspectives and the Northern Ireland Conflict* (pp. 272–288). Edinburgh & London: Mainstream.

Darby, J., & Williamson, A. (Eds.) (1978). *Violence and the Social Services in Northern Ireland*. London: Heinemann.

DEL (2003). *Department for Employment and Learning Compendium of Northern Ireland Education Statistics 1990–1991 to 2002–2003*. Belfast: DEL.

Deutsch, R., & McGowan, V. (1973). *Northern Ireland, 1968–1973: A Chronology of Events*. Belfast: Blackstaff.

DHSS(NI) (1998). *Living with the Trauma of the Troubles*, Belfast: DHSS(NI).

DHSSPS (2002). *Counselling in Northern Ireland: Report of the Counselling Review*. Belfast: DHSSPS.

DHSSPS (2002a). *Report of the Healing Through Remembering Project*. Belfast: DHSSPS.

Ekins, R. (1991). Psychoanalysis and psychoanalytic psychotherapy training in Northern Ireland. *British Journal of Psychotherapy, 8*(2): 199–201.

Farren, S., & Mulvihill, R. F. (2000). *Paths to a Settlement : Great Britain*: Colin Smythe.

Fay, M. T, Morrissey, M., & Smyth, M. (1999). *Northern Ireland's Troubles: The Human Costs*. London: Pluto.

Freud, S. (1921c). Group psychology and the analysis of the ego. *S.E., 18*. London: Hogarth Press.

Gabbard, G. O. (2000). *Psychodynamic Psychiatry in Clinical Practice* (3rd edn). Washington: American Psychiatric Press.

Gaffikin, F., & Morrissey, M. (1990). *Northern Ireland: The Thatcher Years.* London: Pluto.

Gallagher, A. M., & Smith, A. (2000). *The effects of the system of selective secondary education in Northern Ireland.* Bangor: Department of Education for Northern Ireland.

Gibson, M. (1996). The Kegworth experience. In: *Journeys of Experience* (pp. 56–72). London: National Institute of Social Work.

Goleman, D. (1996). *Emotional Intelligence: Why it can Matter More than IQ.* London: Bloomsbury.

Gooch, S. (1991). Infantile sexuality revisited: the agony and ecstasy of the mother–infant couple. *Journal of The Academy of Psychoanalysis, 19*(2): 245–270.

Gormley-Heenan, C., & Robinson, G. (2003). Political leadership: protagonists and pragmatists in Northern Ireland. In: O. Hargie & D. Dickson (Eds.), *Researching the Troubles: Social Science Perspectives and the Northern Ireland Conflict* (pp. 259–272). Edinburgh & London: Mainstream.

Greenson, R. R. (1967). *The Technique and Practice of Psychoanalysis.* New York: International Universities Press.

Grinberg, L., Sor, D., & DeBianchedi, E. T. (1975). *Introduction to the Work of Bion.* Perthshire: Clunie.

Grossman, D. (1996). *On Killing: The Psychological Cost of Learning to Kill in War and Society.* Boston: Little Brown.

Hainsworth, P. (1998). *Divided Society: Ethnic Minorities and Racism in Northern Ireland.* London: Pluto.

Hamber, B. (Ed.) (1998). *Past Imperfect: Dealing with the Past in Northern Ireland and Societies in Transition.* Derry: Incore.

Hamber, B., & Wilson, R. (2002). Symbolic closure through memory, reparation and revenge in post-conflict societies. *Journal of Human Rights, 1*(1).

Hamber, B., Nageng, D., & O'Malley, G. (2000). Telling it like it is: understanding the Truth and Reconciliation Commission from the perspective of survivors. *Psychology in Society, 26*: 18–42.

Hargie, O., & Dickson, D. (Eds.) *Researching the Troubles: Social Science Perspectives and the Northern Ireland Conflict.* Edinburgh & London: Mainstream.

Harlow, H. (1961). The development of affectional patterns in infant monkeys. In: B. M. Foss (Ed.), *Determinants of Infant Behaviour* (pp. 75–97). New York: John Wiley.

Hayes, P., & Campbell, J. (2000). The psychological sequelae and state response to Bloody Sunday. *Research on Social Work Practice, 10*(6): 705–720.

Heenan, D., & Lloyd, K. (2002). Housing and social exclusion. In: A. M. Gray, K. Lloyd, P. Devine, G. Robinson, & D. Heenan (Eds.), *Social Attitudes in Northern Ireland: the 8th Report* (pp. 102–119). London: Pluto.

Heimann, P. (1956). Dynamics of transference interpretations. *International Journal of Psychoanalysis, 37*: 303–310.

Herman, J. L. (1992). *Trauma and Recovery.* Basic Books: London.

Heskin, K. (1980). *Northern Ireland: A Psychological Analysis.* Dublin: Gill and Macmillan.

Hinshelwood, R. D. (1989). *A Dictionary of Kleinian Thought.* New York: Jason Aronson.

HMSO (2003). *Social Trends 34.* London: HMSO.

Holmes, J. (2001). *Ideas in Psychoanalysis: Narcissism.* Cambridge: Icon Books.

Hughes, T. (1997). *Tales from Ovid.* London: Faber & Faber.

HURT Victims Support Group (2001). *The Forgotten Victims.* Island Pamphlets. Regency Press: Belfast.

Jarman, N. (2003) Managing disorder: responses to interface violence in Northern Belfast. In: O. Hargie & D. Dickson (Eds.), *Researching the Troubles: Social Science Perspectives and the Northern Ireland Conflict* (pp. 227–244). Edinburgh & London: Mainstream.

Joseph, B. (1982). Addiction to near death. *International Journal of Psychoanalysis. 63*, 449–56.

Joseph, B. (1986) Envy in everyday life. *Psychoanalytic Psychotherapy,* 2: 13–22 [reprinted in: M. Feldman & E. G. Spillius (Eds.), *Psychic Equilibrium and Psychic Change.* London: Routledge, 1989, pp. 181–191].

Joseph, B. (1989). The patient who is difficult to reach. In: M. Feldman & E. B. Spillius (Eds.), *Psychic Equilibrium and Psychic Change* (pp. 75–87). London: Routledge.

Kaminer, D., Stein, D. J., Mbarga, I., & Zungu-Dirwayi, N. (2001). The Truth and Reconciliation Commission in South Africa. Relation to psychiatric status and forgiveness among survivors of human rights abuses. *British Journal of Psychiatry, 178*: 373–377.

Kapur, R. (2001). Omagh: The Beginning of the Reparative Impulse? *Psychoanalytic Psychotherapy, 15*, (3), p. 265–278. Also in: Covington, C., Wilhams, P., Arundale, J. & Knox, J. (2002). *Terrorism and War:*

Unconscious Dynamics of Political Violence. London and New York: Karnac, P. 315–328.

Kapur, R. (2002). A troubled mind afraid to talk: group therapy in Northern Ireland (unpublished).

Kapur, R. (2004). Dealing with damage: the desire for psychic violence to soothe psychic pain. *International Journal of Psychoanalysis* (submitted).

Kapur, R., & Campbell, J. (2002). The troubled mind of Northern Ireland: social care, object relations theory and political conflict. *Journal of Social Work Practice, 16*(1): 67–76.

Kapur, R., Weir, M., McKevitt, C., Collins, L., Maxwell, H., & Heany, C. (1997). An evaluation of Threshold's therapeutic communities in Northern Ireland. *Irish Journal of Psychological Medicine, 14*(2): 65–68.

Kernberg, O. F. (2003a). Sanctioned social violence: a psychoanalytic view—Part I. *International Journal of Psychoanalysis, 84*(3): 683–698.

Kernberg, O. F. (2003b). Sanctioned social violence: a psychoanalytic view—Part II. *International Journal of Psychoanalysis, 84*(4): 953–968.

Klein, M. (1921). 'Eine Kinderentwicklung', *Imago*, 270, and in translation as The development of a child. *International Journal of Psychoanalysis, IV*: 419–474.

Klein, M. (1926). Infant analysis. *International Journal of Psychoanalysis, VII*: 31–63.

Klein, M. (1927). Criminal tendencies in normal children. *British Journal of Medical Psychology, V*(11): 177–192.

Klein, M. (1928). Early stages of the Oedipus conflict. *International Journal of Psychoanalysis, IX*: 167–180.

Klein, M. (1932). *The Psychoanalysis of Children*. London: Hogarth Press.

Klein, M. (1935). A contribution to the psychogenesis of manic depressive states. *International Journal of Psychoanalysis, XVI*: 145–174.

Klein, M. (1940). Mourning and its relation to manic depressive states. *International Journal of Psychoanalysis, XXI*: 125–53.

Klein, M. (1946). Notes on some schizoid mechanisms. *International Journal of Psychoanalysis, XXII*: 99–110 [reprinted in: J. Mitchell (Ed.), *The Selected Melanie Klein* (pp. 175–200), New York: Free Press, 1986].

Krishnamurti, J. (1983). In: H. Lutyens (Ed.), *Krishnamurti The Years of Fulfilment*. London: J. Murry.

Loughry, G. C., Bell, P., Kee, M., Roddy, R. J., & Curran, P. S. (1988). Post-traumatic disorder and civil violence in Northern Ireland. *British Journal of Psychiatry, 153*: 554–560.

Lyons, H. A. (1974). Terrorist bombing and the psychological sequelae. *Journal of the Irish Medical Association, 65*: 15.

McGarry, J. (Ed.) (2001). *Northern Ireland and the Divided World—Post-Agreement Northern Ireland in Comparative Perspective*. Oxford: Oxford University Press.

McGarry, J., & O'Leary, B. (1996). *Explaining Northern Ireland*. Oxford: Blackwell.

McVeigh, R. (1997)[1995] Cherishing the children of the nation unequally: sectarianism in Ireland. In: P. Clancy, S. Drudy, K. Lynch, & L. O'Dowd (Eds.), *Irish Society: Sociological Perspectives* (pp. 620–651). Dublin: IPA.

Meltzer, D. (1973). *Sexual States of Mind*. Perthshire. Clunie Press.

Menzies Lyth, I. (1988). *Containing Anxiety in Institutions—Selected Essays*, Volume 1. London: Free Association Books.

Milgram, S. (1963). Behavioural study of obedience. *Journal of Abnormal and Social Psychology, 67*: 371–378.

Mitchell, J. (Ed.) (1986). *The Selected Melanie Klein*. New York: Free Press.

Mitrani, J. L. (2001). *Ordinary People and Extra-Ordinary Projections: A Post-Kleinian Approach to the Treatment of Primitive Mental States*. London and New York: Routledge.

Morrissey, M., & Smyth, M. (2002). *Northern Ireland after the Good Friday Agreement: Victims, Grievance and Blame*. London: Pluto.

Morrow, D., Eyben, K., & Wilson, D. (2003). From the margin to the middle: taking equity, diversity and interdependence seriously. In: O. Hargie & D. Dickson, (Eds.), *Researching the Troubles: Social Science Perspectives and the Northern Ireland Conflict* (pp. 163–182). Edinburgh & London: Mainstream.

Murtagh, G. (2003). Territorality, research and policy making in Northern Ireland. In: O. Hargie & D. Dickson (Eds.), *Researching the Troubles: Social Science Perspectives and the Northern Ireland Conflict* (pp. 227–244). Edinburgh & London: Mainstream.

Northern Ireland Abstract of Statistics (2003). Belfast: NISRA.

Northern Ireland Office (1998a). *The Agreement* (Belfast, HMSO).

O'Dowd, L., Rolston, B., & Tomlinson, M. (1980). *Northern Ireland: Between Civil Rights and Civil War*. London: CSE Books.

Office of the First and Deputy First Minister for Northern Ireland (2002). *Reshape, Rebuild, Achieve*. Belfast: OFDFM.

Pinkerton, J. & Campbell, J. (2002). Social work and social justice in Northern Ireland: towards a new occupational space. *British Journal of Social Work, 33*: 723–737.

Reich, W. (1949) *Character Analysis*. New York: Orgone Institute Press.

Rice, C. A., & Kapur, R. (2002). The impact of the "Troubles" on therapy groups in Northern Ireland. *Group, 26*(3): 247–264.

Riesenberg-Malcolm, R. (1999). *On Bearing Unbearable States of Mind.* London and New York: Routledge.

Rolston, B., & Miller, D. (Eds.) (1996). *War and Words: The Northern Ireland Media Reader.* Belfast: Beyond the Pale.

Rosenfeld, H.R. (1987) *Impasse and Interpretation: Therapeutic and Antitherapeutic Facts in the Psychoanalytic Treatment of Psychotic, Borderline and Neurotic Patients.* Hove, E. Sussex & NewYork: Brunner-Routledge.

Rowan, B. (2003). *The Armed Peace: Life and Death After the Ceasefires.* Edinburgh & London: Mainstream.

Rustin, M. (1991). *The Good Society and the Inner Worth: Psychoanalysis, Politics and Culture.* London and New York: Verso.

Segal, H. (1973). *Introduction to the Work of Melanie Klein.* London: Hogarth Press.

Segal, H. (1981/85). *The Work of Hannah Segal: A Kleinian Approach to Clinical Practice.* London: Free Association & Maresfield Library.

Segal, H. (1995). In: A. Elliott & S. Frosh (Eds.), *Psychoanalysis in Contexts* (pp. 191–204). London & New York: Routledge.

Sinnerton, H. (2002). *David Ervine: Unchartered Waters.* Dingle, Ireland: Brandon.

Smyth, M., & Campbell, J. (1996). Social work, sectarianism and anti-sectarian practice in Northern Ireland. *British Journal of Social Work,* 26: 77–92.

Smyth, M., Morrissey, M., & Hamilton, J. (2001). *Caring Through the Troubles: Health and Social Services in North and West Belfast.* Belfast: North and West Belfast Health and Social Services Trust.

Spillius, E. B. (1988a). *Melanie Klein Today: Developments in Theory and Practice. Vol. 1: Mainly Theory.* London and New York. Routledge.

Spillius, E. B. (1988b). *Melanie Klein Today: Developments in Theory and Practice. Vol. 2. Mainly Practice.* London and New York: Routledge.

Spitz, R. A. (1962). Autoeroticism re-examined. The role of early sexual behaviour patterns in personality formation: *Psychoanalytic Study Child,* 17: 283–315.

Steiner, J. (1993). *Psychic Retreats.* London: Routledge.

Stone, M. (2003). *None Shall Divide Us.* GB: John Blake.

Sugden, J., & Bairner, A. (1993). *Sport, Sectarianism and Society in a Divided Ireland.* Leicester: Leicester University Press.

Teague, P. (1993). Discrimination and fair employment in Northern Ireland. In: P. Teague (Ed.), *The Economy of Northern Ireland: Perspectives for Structural Change* (pp. 141–169.). London: Lawrence & Wishart.

The Independent (1995). 12 July.

Van der Kolk, B. S., & Van der Hart, O. (1989). Pierre Janet and the breakdown of adaptation in psychological trauma. *American Journal of Psychiatry. 146*: 1530–1540.

Volkan, V. D. (1999). Individual and large-group identity: parallels in development and characteristics in stability and crisis. *Croatian Medical Journal, 40*(3): 458–465.

Whyte, J. (1991). *Interpreting Northern Ireland.* Oxford: Clarendon.

Wilson, J. P. (1989). *Trauma, Transformation and Healing: An Integrative Approach to Theory, Research and Post-traumatic Therapy.* New York: Brunner-Mazel.

Winnicott, D. W. (1979). *The Maturational Process and the Facilitating Environment.* London: Hogarth.

Wittenberg, I. (1997). Autism as a defence against hopelessness. In: J. Mitrani & T. Mitrani, (Eds.), *Encounters with Autistic States* (pp. 125–142). Northvale, NJ:Jason Aronson.

Wright, F. (1996). *The Banner of Ulster* (1852). In: *Two Lands on One Soil; Ulster Politicals before Home Rule* (p. 202). Dublin: Gill & Macmillan.

Yalom, I. R. (1985). *The Theory and Practice of Group Psychotherapy.* New York: Karnac.

GLOSSARY

This glossary does not aim to be comprehensive. For a more detailed account of Kleinian terminology see Hinshelwood, R. (1991), *A Dictionary of Kleinian Thought*.

Anxiety This is mainly considered to be the manifestation of the death instinct or destructive impulses. It takes two main forms, depressive anxiety and paranoid anxiety (see below).

Bad or persecuting object is where bad and hostile experiences are projected into someone or something that becomes the source of persecution.

Castration anxiety refers to the fear, particularly of males, of being cut off. This may either be in reality, with little boys fearing the loss of their penis, or adult men fearing "put downs", humiliation, and ridicule.

Coupling usually refers to the image we have of our parental coupling. This may be of a benevolent, kind, combined couple, particularly in the "primal scene" of sexual intercourse *or* a more malevolent, cruel, and paranoid coupling aimed at destructive attacks. This mental blueprint has a critical influence on how we conduct our day-to-day lives.

Depressive anxiety is the worry that one's own hostility will annihilate and destroy the good object. It is part of the depressive position, where there is a capacity for concern that the object that has been attacked will be damaged.

Depressive position has also been called the capacity for concern, where there is a guilt about how the other person has been treated if a destructive act, by word or deed, has occurred. Here the other person is seen as a "whole object" or total person with thoughts and feelings rather than a "part object" or someone devoid of human feelings.

Envy is a critical concept in understanding human destructiveness. Like a terrorist, envy attacks without notice, leaves its trauma and often disappears without being brought to justice. As it is a deeply hidden and well disguised act, it can cause emotional havoc with no personal responsibility taken. Invariably only "voluntary guilt" can allow the person to move from envy to greater emotional maturity.

Good object In the depressive position this is felt to be a source of life, love, and goodness, but is not ideal. There is a realistic appraisal of this good objective in that it is more good than bad. It is also felt to be vulnerable to attacks and, therefore, is often experienced as damaged or destroyed.

Guilt This can be either reparative or persecuting. Fundamentally it refers to a feeling of having damaged people with harsh, cruel words and unjust actions.

Idealization Here all good abilities and traits are projected into the other person. Perfection and the absence of badness is characteristic of this state of mind. There is an unrealistic and glorified appraisal of the other person who is "put on a pedestal". This is often a defence against hatred and envy of the idealized person.

Ideal objects For the infant this is usually, in phantasy, expressed as an attachment to the breast as an idealized experience, e.g., bountiful breast.

Internal world is a description of our inner phantasies and images of ourselves and others. We take in or introject experiences which make up our feelings and thoughts about ourselves. Good mental health is about internalizing more positive than negative experiences and so holding on to a set of good internal objects or representations about ourselves and others.

Manic defences highlight a style of human relationships characterized by triumph, control and contempt. The saying "empty vessels make loud noises" refers to the hollowness of a person who uses superiority and status to "get one over" on others.

Oedipus Complex For boys, the rival is the father for mother's affections (Oedipus Complex) and for girls, the mother is the rival for father's affections (Electra Complex). If these rivalries are unresolved, people act out their rivalry with others with the unconscious aim of securing the affections of the opposite sexed parent or authority figure. Someone who has failed to resolve this conflict will find it difficult to accept thirdness; an idea that another person can exist in a two-way relationship.

Paranoid anxiety or persecutory anxiety refers to the fear that projected hostility or destructiveness will annihilate the person by returning the hostility with acts of persecution. In other words, "the empire strikes back" in this "paranoid–schizoid" position.

Paranoid–schizoid position This state of mind is primarily characterized by hostility and suspicion and a withdrawal from relationships. People are experienced as "part-objects" or "things" rather than whole human beings.

Part objects Refers either to the dehumanization of people as numbers or things and how positive or negative feelings can be attached to male or female genitalia, i.e. penis or breast/vagina.

Persecutory guilt refers to the self blame and inner torment when relationships break down. This is part of the paranoid–schizoid position where there is little internal benevolence and understanding.

Projection and projective identification Projection is where good or bad feelings are put *on to* another person, usually by means of words or some visible act. Projective identification is where feelings are put *into* another person without words; here "gut feelings" become the source and receiving point for communications.

Psychic reality This is the experience of our internal worlds. To achieve psychic truth is to disentangle reality from projections that we put into other people, so that an objective reality free of distorting phantasies can be achieved.

Reparation This act of reparative guilt is critical for healing and positive human relationships. This has to be differentiated from manic reparation where there is a cosmetic and false act of making good a destructive act. An example of manic reparation could be showering someone with gifts when deep down you don't feel sorry for what has been done.

Reparative guilt is part of the depressive position and refers to the painful realization of having damaged others. This initiates the realization that others are human beings, with thoughts and feelings and are worthy of being treated more humanely.

Splitting There are two forms of splitting. First, there is the splitting of experiences in absolute terms either into all bad *or* all good, with no integration of both. Next there is the splitting off of bad and good feelings, in phantasy, which are then projected into the other person. Good mental health, in the depressive position, is about integrating good and bad experiences *and* retrieving good and bad projections that have been located elsewhere.

Whole objects Here people are seen as whole human beings who are also fathers, mothers, sons, daughters, etc., so diffusing hatred and allowing a humanization of negative processes. Whole-object relatedness requires considerable thought and care to treat others as human beings.

INDEX